Poems
of
Lewis
Carroll

Poems
of
Lewis Carroll

SELECTED BY
Myra Cohn Livingston

*With illustrations by John Tenniel, Harry Furniss,
Henry Holiday, Arthur B. Frost, and Lewis Carroll
from the original editions*

THOMAS Y. CROWELL COMPANY   NEW YORK

Designed by Angela Foote

Manufactured in the United States of America

ISBN 0–690–00178–9

1 2 3 4 5 6 7 8 9 10

Library of Congress Cataloging in Publication Data
Dodgson, Charles Lutwidge, 1832–1898.
    Poems of Lewis Carroll.
    (The Crowell poets)
    I. Livingston, Myra Cohn, ed.   II. Title.
PR4611.A4L5   821'.8   73–7914
ISBN 0–690–00178–9

The Crowell Poets
Under the Editorship of Lillian Morrison

Contents

Introduction

Anyone who has met Alice, the Cheshire Cat, the Mad Hatter—the dozens of animals and personages who spill over Wonderland—has caught a glimpse (perhaps unwittingly) of a delightful Victorian gentleman by the name of Charles Lutwidge Dodgson. Far better recognized by his pen name, Lewis Carroll, he is known throughout the world as the creator of *Alice's Adventures in Wonderland, Through the Looking-Glass, and What Alice Found There;* and unparalleled nonsense verse.

The same man who dreamed up the Jabberwock and the Bandersnatch also invented mathematical and word puzzles, cipher methods and games of logic. The Dodgson who enjoyed croquet, chess, and billiards was a devotee of the arts—singing, painting, and most particularly the theatre. He was an outstanding and recognized photographer. A deacon of the Church of England, a resident of Christ Church, an Oxford college, he taught mathematics for over a quarter of a century. He was elected to the Curatorship of the Common Room of that college for ten years, where he involved himself with ordering wines and mineral waters, bookkeeping, and servants' wages. The Lewis Carroll who wrote the *Alice* books also wrote mathematical treatises, pamphlets on local affairs and politics, and invented such games as Doublets, Lanrick, Circular Billiards, and Syzygies, as well as elaborate rules for lawn tennis tournaments. The same Dodgson who carried a black bag filled with puzzles, games, and sleight-of-hand tricks to amuse the children he might meet on railway journeys, who kept in his pocket a supply of safety pins for any little girls at the seashore who might wish to pin up their dresses and wade in the surf, who treated children to the theatre and trips to the seashore, was also the deeply religious man who confided to his diary on February 14, 1871, "A working life is a happy one, but oh that mine were better and nearer to God!"

There seemed never enough hours for Dodgson's diversified interests. He entertained friends in his rooms at Christ Church, taking care that no guest should be served the same menu twice. He took long walks, often as much as twenty miles a day, journeyed to the seashore, to art galleries, to friends' homes, and to the theatre. (The "true end and object of acting," he wrote in 1855, is "to raise the mind above itself, and out of petty everyday cares.") The photography of his day was a complicated affair, demanding as to equipment, time, and patience. To carry about his paraphernalia, to involve himself with the complicated process (somewhat described in his parody "Hiawatha's Photographing"), and to meet his own meticulous standards of excellence were no mean accomplishments. Yet even today his portraiture is considered outstanding.

Dodgson's correspondence alone kept him writing, by his own estimate, some 2000 letters a year at least, and he kept a letter registry noting the correspondent and brief details of the contents of each letter. Some 98,721 letters had been carefully recorded just before his death. It is not surprising that he also wrote "Eight or Nine Wise Words About Letter Writing" and invented a stamp case to go with it.

He was, as might be expected, a perfectionist. His letters to his illustrators, John Tenniel, Henry Holiday, Harry Furniss, and to Macmillan, his publisher, showed no compromise in his insistence upon quality and attention to detail. An advertisement which he distributed in 1893 is typical: "For over 25 years," he wrote, "I have made it my chief object, with regard to my books, that they should be of the best workmanship attainable for the price. And I am deeply annoyed to find that the last issue of 'Through the Looking-Glass' . . . has been put on sale without its being noticed that most of the pictures have failed so much in the printing, as to make the book not worth buying." Dodgson instructed all those who held such books to return them to his publishers and exchange them for the next issue. "Instead, however, of destroying the unsold copies, I propose to utilise them by giving them away, to Mechanics' Institutes, Village Reading-Rooms, and similar institutions, where the means for purchasing such books are scanty. Accordingly I invite applications for such gifts. . . ."

The world of reality, the world of imagination—neither escaped the humor, the satire, the parody of Lewis Carroll's pen. The *Alice* books are unique, but not alone. Four books of poetry

—Phantasmagoria, The Hunting of the Snark, Rhyme? and Reason? and *Three Sunsets*—appeared during his lifetime, ranging from serious poetry to the most biting of parody and burlesque. *Sylvie and Bruno* and *Sylvie and Bruno Concluded, A Nursery "Alice,"* and *The Game of Logic* were written for children. He published a large number of treatises on mathematics—foremost among them being *Euclid and His Modern Rivals,* an amusing but serious argument favoring a revised Euclid above other modern substitutes for the study of elementary geometry—and both serious and humorous pamphlets on academic matters.

Charles Lutwidge Dodgson was born January 27, 1832, at Daresbury, Cheshire, England, the eldest son of the eleven children of the Reverend Charles Dodgson and Jane Lutwidge Dodgson. As a child he played with his sisters, learning sleight-of-hand tricks, helping to construct marionettes and a marionette theatre, and writing the plays himself. He devised a "railway" game, the train made from a wheelbarrow, barrel, and small truck, complete with "refreshment stations" and elaborate rules. At thirteen he wrote his first "book," *Useful and Instructive Poetry.* At Croft, where the Dodgsons moved in 1843, family magazines flourished, and he copied into *The Rectory Magazine, The Rectory Umbrella* and *Mischmasch* his contributions—verse, parodies, stories, and articles. At twelve he was sent to the Richmond School in Yorkshire; the following year he wrote his first book, *Useful and Instructive Poetry.* From 1846–1850 he attended Rugby. He matriculated at Christ Church, Oxford, in 1850 and came into residence in 1851, the year of his mother's death. After winning numerous honors, he received his B.A. and became a "Master of the House" in 1855. He received his M.A. in 1857. These years saw the beginning of his verse contributions to *College Rhymes, The Whitby Gazette, The Comic Times, Punch,* and *The Train.* It was the editor of *The Train,* Edmund

Yates, who suggested he choose a *nom de plume*. Although Dodgson suggested four names, Yates chose one that was a variant on Dodgson's two Christian names: Lewis = Ludovicus = Lutwidge and Carroll = Carolus = Charles. His use of the initials B. B. and R. W. G. for poems published in *College Rhymes* has never been explained.

Dodgson lived at Christ Church for forty-seven years, except for one summer trip abroad and frequent trips to the seashore. He often visited his family at Croft, and later at Guildford, where his sisters moved after their father's death in 1868. He served as Mathematical Lecturer for twenty-six years, from 1855 to 1881, and was ordained a deacon in 1861.

The diaries he kept give evidence of a man whose days fluctuated between hard work and joyous recreation, days given to lecturing, tutorial duties, gatherings at a friend's home, excursions to galleries, to see a play, days of writing, reading, days when he would entertain or go visiting. Days of special interest, or days on which he might meet someone exciting to him, were recorded with the Latin *Dies notabilis* (notable day) or *Dies mirabilis* (wonderful day) or oftentimes, "I mark this day with a white stone." As a fellow at a great Oxford college, he was in a position to meet the celebrities of his day. Tennyson, Thackeray, George MacDonald, John Ruskin, he knew and photographed. Yet, he chided himself continually, as in this entry of December 21, 1863:

> Here, at the close of another year, how much of neglect, carelessness, and sin have I to remember! I had hoped, during the year, to have made a beginning in parochial work, to have thrown off habits of evil, to have advanced in my work at Christ Church. How little, next to nothing, has been done of all this! Now I have a fresh year

before me: once more let me set myself to do something worthy of life "before I go hence, and be no more seen" . . . .

Much has been written about Lewis Carroll. The *Alice* books and *The Hunting of the Snark* have long been fertile field for the "message-hunters," allegory and symbol seekers. Those who asked Dodgson to explain the meaning behind such a poem as the *Snark*, were told that such an explanation was impossible: "Are you able to explain things which you don't yourself understand?" he wrote to a child-friend, Mary Brown, in 1880. On the other hand, he delighted in explaining the makeup of his portmanteau words ("where there are two meanings packed into one word"). Three years earlier he had written to another child-friend, Maud Standen, about his "Jabberwock" poem: "I am afraid I can't explain 'vorpal blade' for you—nor yet 'tulgey wood'; but I did make an explanation once for 'uffish thought'— It seems to suggest a state of mind when the voice is gruffish, the manner roughish, and the temper huffish. Then again, as to 'burble': if you take the three verbs 'bleat,' 'murmur' and 'warble,' and select the bits I have underlined, it certainly *makes* 'burble': though I am afraid I can't distinctly remember having made it that way." The nearest that Dodgson himself ever came to satisfying queries as to "meanings" occur in his "Stanza of Anglo-Saxon Poetry" and in the conversation between Alice and Humpty Dumpty in *Through the Looking-Glass*. The preface to *The Hunting of the Snark* and Dodgson's various inscriptions in copies he gave to his child-friends offer possible clues. But perhaps better than all the commentaries are his own letters and diaries. One can glean much about the creator of *Alice* from such a letter as he wrote to Sydney Bowles (Lady Redesdale) in 1891, just six years before his death:

"In *some* ways, you know, people that *don't* exist, are much nicer than people that *do*. For instance, people that *don't* exist are never *cross:* and they never *contradict* you: and *they never tread on your toes!* Oh, they're ever so much nicer than people that *do* exist!"

Charles L. Dodgson was a shy man, a man who avoided publicity, and whose handicaps—a bad stammer and one deaf ear—made him far more comfortable with his child-friends. "Much of the brightness of my life, and it has been a wonderfully happy one," wrote Dodgson in 1894, "has come from the friendship of girlfriends. Twenty or thirty years ago, 'ten' was about my ideal age for such friends; now 'twenty' or 'twenty-five' is nearer the mark. Some of my dearest child-friends are 30 or more: and I think an old man of 62 has the right to regard them as being 'child-friends' still."

He was also a great tease. "Next time I call," he wrote to Kate Terry Lewis in 1882, "I hope *you'll* be at home: you had gone to the Dentist when I called the other day. Oh! how I envied you when I heard it. A good play, or a gallery of good pictures is a very delightful thing to go to—but a *Dentist,* oh, there are not words (are there?) to describe the delight. . . ."

Boys, he wrote to a friend that same year, "are not an attractive race of beings (as a little boy, I was simply detestable). . . ." Thus he sought the company of girls—Edith, Alice, and Lorina Liddell; Gertrude Chataway; Edith Argles; the Drury sisters; Harriet, Mary, and Ina Watson (for whom he invented the portmanteau name of Harmarina)—including many child-actresses of the day: the Bowman girls, Kate Terry Lewis, Adelaide Paine, and most famous of all, Ellen Terry, a lifelong friend. One of his most memorable friends was, of course, Alice Liddell, for whom he made up the *Alice* books and to whom they were dedicated. The story of the July fourth date in 1862, when he and a friend, the Reverend Robinson Duckworth, took the three Liddell sisters rowing on the Thames River and Dodgson told them the "fairy-tale of Alice's adventures underground" is recorded in his dairy, as well as through the prefatory poem to *Alice's Adventures in Wonderland:*

> *All in the golden afternoon*
> *Full leisurely we glide. . . .*

Alice Liddell was ten years old at the time, and the book that he first wrote in manuscript, *Alice's Adventures Underground,* was later expanded into the book as we know it today. Published in 1865, it was followed by *Through the Looking-Glass, and What Alice Found There* in 1872. What a joy it must have been to children of the Victorian age, accustomed to books of piety and morality, to encounter the White Queen, the Walrus and the Carpenter, the White Rabbit, and the Dodo, to find a story with fun and enjoyment, and didactic poems with their morals and preachments turned into parodies! Dodgson as early as 1855 had lamented that all existing marionette plays were either not suited to children or were "overpoweringly dull" with "no idea of fun in them." Here again is an echo of his devotion to the theatre and to acting, "to raise the mind above itself, and out of petty everyday cares—."

For anyone who has read the works of Lewis Carroll, the diaries, the letters (such as are available), there emerges the picture of a complex, sometimes eccentric man, but a man who left, through his many writings, a biography of himself. The absurdities of the human race he recorded in prose and poetry, using nonsense, based on logic, as his tool. It is only in his serious verse and in the *Sylvie and Bruno* books that Carroll the writer faltered, for here he tried to teach—indeed, to preach—and the results are dull and dreary. Dodgson, the deeply religious man, believed in God and in love, but he differed from orthodox religious views in one essential respect: he could not believe in eternal damnation. His faith offered him endless and joyous possibilities for life.

> I must find a few minutes [he wrote to Kate Terry Lewis in 1893], to offer you the very sincere wishes of an old friend that your married life may be a bright and peaceful one, and that you and your chosen husband may love each other with a love second only to your love of God and far above your love of any other object. For *that* is, I believe, the only *essential* for a happy married life: All else is trivial compared with it. You surely do not *expect* a 'lone, lorn creature' like me—a wretched old bachelor—to cloud the happy day by his sombre presence? You might as well expect a screech-owl to come out in the noon-day and disport himself in your beautiful garden. With an old man's love, I am

> Affectionately yours,
> C. L. Dodgson

If Dodgson struggled with the concept of love, his commitment to God, his deep devotion to his family, his own bachelorhood, he found much of the love that he craved and needed from his child-friends. A letter, probably written to Gertrude Chataway (to whom he dedicated *The Hunting of the Snark*) is indicative:

> Oh child, child! I kept my promise yesterday afternoon, and came down to the sea, to go with you along the rocks: but I saw you going with another gentleman, so I thought I wasn't wanted just yet: so I walked about a bit, and when I got back I couldn't see you anywhere, though I went a good way on the rocks to look. There *was* a child in pink that looked [like] you: but when I got up to her it was the wrong child: however that wasn't *her* fault, poor thing. She

couldn't help being a stranger. So I helped her with her sandcastles, and then I went home. I didn't cry *all* the way.

Your loving friend,
C. L. Dodgson

Charles Lutwidge Dodgson died at Guildford on January 14, 1898, at the age of sixty-five. One stanza, from "Stolen Waters," a serious poem written when he was thirty years old, may well be as autobiographical as ever six lines can be:

Be as a child—
So shalt thou sing for very joy of breath—
So shalt thou wait thy dying,
In holy transport lying—
So pass rejoicing through the gate of death,
In garment undefiled.

In this way did Lewis Carroll live, die, and sing.

Poems

from

Alice's Adventures in Wonderland

and

Through the Looking-Glass, and What Alice Found There

from
Alice's Adventures
in Wonderland

How doth the little crocodile
   Improve his shining tail,
And pour the waters of the Nile
   On every golden scale!

How cheerfully he seems to grin,
   How neatly spreads his claws,
And welcomes little fishes in,
   With gently smiling jaws!

Twinkle, twinkle, little bat!
How I wonder what you're at!
Up above the world you fly,
Like a tea-tray in the sky.
     Twinkle, twinkle——

Fury said to
a mouse, That
he met in the
house, "Let
us both go
to law: *I*
will prose-
cute *you.*—
Come, I'll
take no de-
nial: We
must have
the trial;
For really
this morn-
ing I've
nothing
to do."
Said the
mouse to
the cur,
"Such a
trial, dear
sir, With
no jury
or judge,
would
be wast-
ing our
breath."
"I'll be
judge,
I'll be
jury,"
said
cun-
ning
old
Fury:
"I'll
try
the
whole
cause,
and
con-
demn
you to
death."

Speak roughly to your little boy,
    And beat him when he sneezes:
He only does it to annoy,
    Because he knows it teases.

       Chorus

      Wow!   wow!   wow!

I speak severely to my boy,
    I beat him when he sneezes;
For he can thoroughly enjoy
    The pepper when he pleases!

       Chorus

      Wow!   wow!   wow!

"You are old, father William," the young man said,
    "And your hair has become very white;
And yet you incessantly stand on your head—
    Do you think, at your age, it is right?"

"In my youth," father William replied to his son,
    "I feared it might injure the brain;
But, now that I'm perfectly sure I have none,
    Why, I do it again and again."

"You are old," said the youth, "as I mentioned before,
   And have grown most uncommonly fat;
Yet you turned a back-somersault in at the door—
   Pray, what is the reason of that?"

"In my youth," said the sage, as he shook his grey locks,
   "I kept all my limbs very supple
By the use of this ointment—one shilling the box--
   Allow me to sell you a couple?"

"You are old," said the youth, "and your jaws are too weak
    For anything tougher than suet;
Yet you finished the goose, with the bones and the beak—
    Pray, how did you manage to do it?"

"In my youth," said his father, "I took to the law,
    And argued each case with my wife;
And the muscular strength, which it gave to my jaw,
    Has lasted the rest of my life."

"You are old," said the youth, "one would hardly suppose
  That your eye was as steady as ever;
Yet you balanced an eel on the end of your nose—
  What made you so awfully clever?"

"I have answered three questions, and that is enough,"
  Said his father. "Don't give yourself airs!
Do you think I can listen all day to such stuff?
  Be off, or I'll kick you down-stairs!"

"Will you walk a little faster?" said a whiting to a snail,
"There's a porpoise close behind us, and he's treading on
my tail.
See how eagerly the lobsters and the turtles all advance!
They are waiting on the shingle—will you come and join
the dance?
    Will you, wo'n't you, will you, wo'n't you, will you join
    the dance?
    Will you, wo'n't you, will you, wo'n't you, wo'n't you join
    the dance?

"You can really have no notion how delightful it will be
When they take us up and throw us, with the lobsters, out
to sea!"
But the snail replied "Too far, too far!" and gave a look
askance—
Said he thanked the whiting kindly, but he would not join
the dance.
    Would not, could not, would not, could not, could not
    join the dance.
    Would not, could not, would not, could not, could not
    join the dance.

"What matters it how far we go?" his scaly friend replied.
"There is another shore, you know, upon the other side.
The further off from England the nearer is to France—
Then turn not pale, beloved snail, but come and join
the dance.
    Will you, wo'n't you, will you, wo'n't you, will you join
    the dance?
    Will you, wo'n't you, will you, wo'n't you, wo'n't you join
    the dance?"

'Tis the voice of the Lobster: I heard him declare
"You have baked me too brown, I must sugar my hair."
As a duck with his eyelids, so he with his nose
Trims his belt and his buttons, and turns out his toes.
When the sands are all dry, he is gay as a lark,
And will talk in contemptuous tones of the Shark:
But, when the tide rises and sharks are around,
His voice has a timid and tremulous sound.

I passed by his garden, and marked, with one eye,
How the Owl and the Panther were sharing a pie:
The Panther took pie-crust, and gravy, and meat,
While the Owl had the dish as its share of the treat.
When the pie was all finished, the Owl, as a boon,
Was kindly permitted to pocket the spoon:
While the Panther received knife and fork with a growl,
And concluded the banquet by——

TURTLE SOUP

Beautiful Soup, so rich and green,
Waiting in a hot tureen!
Who for such dainties would not stoop?
Soup of the evening, beautiful Soup!
Soup of the evening, beautiful Soup!
    Beau—ootiful Soo—oop!
    Beau—ootiful Soo—oop!
Soo—oop of the e—e—evening,
    Beautiful, beautiful Soup!

Beautiful Soup! Who cares for fish,
Game, or any other dish?
Who would not give all else for two p
ennyworth only of beautiful Soup?
Pennyworth only of beautiful Soup?
    Beau—ootiful Soo—oop!
    Beau—ootiful Soo—oop!
Soo—oop of the e—e—evening,
    Beautiful, beauti—FUL SOUP!

They told me you had been to her,
    And mentioned me to him:
She gave me a good character,
    But said I could not swim.

He sent them word I had not gone
    (We know it to be true):
If she should push the matter on,
    What would become of you?

I gave her one, they gave him two,
    You gave us three or more;
They all returned from him to you,
    Though they were mine before.

If I or she should chance to be
    Involved in this affair,
He trusts to you to set them free,
    Exactly as we were.

My notion was that you had been
    (Before she had this fit)
An obstacle that came between
    Him, and ourselves, and it.

Don't let him know she liked them best,
    For this must ever be
A secret, kept from all the rest,
    Between yourself and me.

from
Through the Looking-Glass,
and What Alice Found There

"First, the fish must be caught."
That is easy: a baby, I think, could have caught it.
"Next, the fish must be bought."
That is easy: a penny, I think, would have bought it.

"Now cook me the fish!"
That is easy, and will not take more than a minute.
"Let it lie in a dish!"
That is easy, because it already is in it.

"Bring it here! Let me sup!"
It is easy to set such a dish on the table.
"Take the dish-cover up!"
Ah, *that* is so hard that I fear I'm unable!

For it holds it like glue—
Holds the lid to the dish, while it lies in the middle:
Which is easiest to do,
Un-dish-cover the fish, or dishcover the riddle?

Answer:

Get an oyster-knife strong,
Insert it 'twixt cover and dish in the middle;
Then you shall before long
Un-dish-cover the OYSTERS—*dishcover the riddle!*

25

JABBERWOCKY

'Twas brillig, and the slithy toves
    Did gyre and gimble in the wabe:
All mimsy were the borogoves,
    And the mome raths outgrabe.

"Beware the Jabberwock, my son!
    The jaws that bite, the claws that catch!
Beware the Jubjub bird, and shun
    The frumious Bandersnatch!"

He took his vorpal sword in hand:
    Long time the manxome foe he sought—
So rested he by the Tumtum tree,
    And stood awhile in thought.

And, as in uffish thought he stood,
    The Jabberwock, with eyes of flame,
Came whiffling through the tulgey wood,
    And burbled as it came!

One, two! One, two! And through and through
    The vorpal blade went snicker-snack!
He left it dead, and with its head
    He went galumphing back.

"And, hast thou slain the Jabberwock?
    Come to my arms, my beamish boy!
O frabjous day! Callooh! Callay!"
    He chortled in his joy.

'Twas brillig, and the slithy toves
　　Did gyre and gimble in the wabe:
All mimsy were the borogoves,
　　And the mome raths outgrabe.

THE WALRUS AND THE CARPENTER

The sun was shining on the sea,
   Shining with all his might:
He did his very best to make
   The billows smooth and bright—
And this was odd, because it was
   The middle of the night.

The moon was shining sulkily,
   Because she thought the sun
Had got no business to be there
   After the day was done—
"It's very rude of him," she said,
   "To come and spoil the fun!"

The sea was wet as wet could be,
   The sands were dry as dry.
You could not see a cloud, because
   No cloud was in the sky:
No birds were flying overhead—
   There were no birds to fly.

The Walrus and the Carpenter
   Were walking close at hand:
They wept like anything to see
   Such quantities of sand:
"If this were only cleared away,"
   They said, "it would be grand!"

"If seven maids with seven mops
   Swept it for half a year,
Do you suppose," the Walrus said,

"That they could get it clear?"
"I doubt it," said the Carpenter,
    And shed a bitter tear.

"O Oysters, come and walk with us!"
    The Walrus did beseech.
"A pleasant walk, a pleasant talk,
    Along the briny beach:
We cannot do with more than four,
    To give a hand to each."

The eldest Oyster looked at him,
    But never a word he said:
The eldest Oyster winked his eye,
    And shook his heavy head—
Meaning to say he did not choose
    To leave the oyster-bed.

But four young Oysters hurried up,
　All eager for the treat:
Their coats were brushed, their faces washed,
　Their shoes were clean and neat—
And this was odd, because, you know,
　They hadn't any feet.

Four other Oysters followed them,
　And yet another four;
And thick and fast they came at last,
　And more, and more, and more—
All hopping through the frothy waves,
　And scrambling to the shore.

The Walrus and the Carpenter
　Walked on a mile or so,
And then they rested on a rock
　Conveniently low:
And all the little Oysters stood
　And waited in a row.

"The time has come," the Walrus said,
    "To talk of many things:
Of shoes—and ships—and sealing wax—
    Of cabbages—and kings—
And why the sea is boiling hot—
    And whether pigs have wings."

"But wait a bit," the Oysters cried,
    "Before we have our chat;
For some of us are out of breath,
    And all of us are fat!"
"No hurry!" said the Carpenter.
    They thanked him much for that.

"A loaf of bread," the Walrus said,
    "Is what we chiefly need:
Pepper and vinegar besides
    Are very good indeed—
Now, if you're ready, Oysters dear,
    We can begin to feed."

"But not on us!" the Oysters cried,
    Turning a little blue.
"After such kindness, that would be
    A dismal thing to do!"
"The night is fine," the Walrus said,
    "Do you admire the view?"

"It was so kind of you to come!
    And you are very nice!"
The Carpenter said nothing but
    "Cut us another slice.
I wish you were not quite so deaf—
    I've had to ask you twice!"

"It seems a shame," the Walrus said,
    "To play them such a trick.
After we've brought them out so far,
    And made them trot so quick!"
The Carpenter said nothing but
    "The butter's spread too thick!"

"I weep for you," the Walrus said:
    "I deeply sympathize."
With sobs and tears he sorted out
    Those of the largest size,
Holding his pocket-handkerchief
    Before his streaming eyes.

"O Oysters," said the Carpenter,
    "You've had a pleasant run!
Shall we be trotting home again?"
    But answer came there none—
And this was scarcely odd, because
    They'd eaten every one.

In winter, when the fields are white,
I sing this song for your delight—

In spring, when woods are getting green,
I'll try and tell you what I mean:

In summer, when the days are long,
Perhaps you'll understand the song:

In autumn, when the leaves are brown,
Take pen and ink, and write it down.

I sent a message to the fish:
I told them "This is what I wish."

The little fishes of the sea,
They sent an answer back to me.

The little fishes' answer was
"We cannot do it, Sir, because—"

I sent to them again to say
"It will be better to obey."

The fishes answered, with a grin,
"Why, what a temper you are in!"

I told them once, I told them twice:
They would not listen to advice.

I took a kettle large and new,
Fit for the deed I had to do.

My heart went hop, my heart went thump:
I filled the kettle at the pump.

Then some one came to me and said
"The little fishes are in bed."

I said to him, I said it plain,
"Then you must wake them up again."

I said it very loud and clear:
I went and shouted in his ear.

But he was very stiff and proud:
He said "You needn't shout so loud!"

And he was very proud and stiff:
He said "I'd go and wake them, if—"

I took a corkscrew from the shelf:
I went to wake them up myself.

And when I found the door was locked,
I pulled and pushed and kicked and knocked.

And when I found the door was shut,
I tried to turn the handle, but—

THE AGED AGED MAN

I'll tell thee everything I can:
    There's little to relate.
I saw an aged aged man,
    A-sitting on a gate.
"Who are you, aged man?" I said.
    "And how is it you live?"
And his answer trickled through my head,
    Like water through a sieve.

He said "I look for butterflies
    That sleep among the wheat:
I make them into mutton-pies,
    And sell them in the street.
I sell them unto men," he said,
    "Who sail on stormy seas;
And that's the way I get my bread—
    A trifle, if you please."

But I was thinking of a plan
    To dye one's whiskers green,
And always use so large a fan
    That they could not be seen.
So, having no reply to give
    To what the old man said,
I cried, "Come, tell me how you live!"
    And thumped him on the head.

His accents mild took up the tale:
    He said "I go my ways,
And when I find a mountain-rill,
    I set it in a blaze;

And thence they make a stuff they call
   Rowland's Macassar-Oil—
Yet twopence-halfpenny is all
   They give me for my toil."

But I was thinking of a way
   To feed oneself on batter,
And so go on from day to day
   Getting a little fatter.
I shook him well from side to side,
   Until his face was blue:
"Come, tell me how you live," I cried,
   "And what it is you do!"

He said "I hunt for haddocks' eyes
   Among the heather bright,
And work them into waistcoat-buttons
   In the silent night.
And these I do not sell for gold
   Or coin of silvery shine,
But for a copper halfpenny,
   And that will purchase nine.

"I sometimes dig for buttered rolls,
   Or set limed twigs for crabs:
I sometimes search the grassy knolls
   For wheels of Hansom-cabs.
And that's the way" (he gave a wink)
   "By which I get my wealth—
And very gladly will I drink
   Your Honour's noble health."

I heard him then, for I had just
   Completed my design

To keep the Menai bridge from rust
    By boiling it in wine.
I thanked him much for telling me
    The way he got his wealth,
But chiefly for his wish that he
    Might drink my noble health.

And now, if e'er by chance I put
    My fingers into glue,
Or madly squeeze a right-hand foot
    Into a left-hand shoe,
Or if I drop upon my toe
    A very heavy weight,
I weep, for it reminds me so
Of that old man I used to know—
Whose look was mild, whose speech was slow,
Whose hair was whiter than the snow,
Whose face was very like a crow,
With eyes, like cinders, all aglow,
Who seemed distracted with his woe,
Who rocked his body to and fro,
And muttered mumblingly and low,
As if his mouth were full of dough,
Who snorted like a buffalo——
That summer evening long ago,
    A-sitting on a gate.

Hush-a-by lady, in Alice's lap!
Till the feast's ready, we've time for a nap.
When the feast's over, we'll go to the ball—
Red Queen, and White Queen, and Alice, and all!

To the Looking-Glass world it was Alice that said
"I've a sceptre in hand, I've a crown on my head.
Let the Looking-Glass creatures, whatever they be
Come and dine with the Red Queen, the White Queen, and me!"

Chorus

Then fill up the glasses as quick as you can,
And sprinkle the table with buttons and bran:
Put cats in the coffee, and mice in the tea—
And welcome Queen Alice with thirty-times-three!

"O Looking-Glass creatures," quoth Alice, "draw near!
'Tis an honour to see me, a favour to hear:
'Tis a privilege high to have dinner and tea
Along with the Red Queen, the White Queen, and me!"

Chorus

Then fill up the glasses with treacle and ink,
Or anything else that is pleasant to drink:
Mix sand with the cider, and wool with the wine—
And welcome Queen Alice with ninety-times-nine!

Poems

from

Sylvie and Bruno

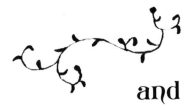

and

Sylvie and Bruno
Concluded

from
Sylvie and Bruno

He thought he saw an Elephant,
   That practised on a fife:
He looked again, and found it was
   A letter from his wife.
"At length I realise," he said,
   "The bitterness of Life!"

He thought he saw a Buffalo
   Upon the chimney-piece:
He looked again, and found it was
   His Sister's Husband's Niece.
"Unless you leave this house," he said,
   "I'll send for the Police!"

He thought he saw a Rattlesnake
 That questioned him in Greek:
He looked again, and found it was
 The Middle of Next Week.
"The one thing I regret," he said,
 "Is that it cannot speak!"

He thought he saw a Banker's Clerk
 Descending from the bus:
He looked again, and found it was
 A Hippopotamus:
"If this should stay to dine," he said,
 "There won't be much for us!"

He thought he saw a Kangaroo
    That worked a coffee-mill:
He looked again, and found it was
    A Vegetable-Pill.
"Were I to swallow this," he said,
    "I should be very ill!"

He thought he saw a Coach-and-Four
    That stood beside his bed:
He looked again, and found it was
    A Bear without a Head.
"Poor thing," he said, "poor silly thing!
    "It's waiting to be fed!"

He thought he saw an Albatross
    That fluttered round the lamp:
He looked again, and found it was
    A Penny-Postage-Stamp.
"You'd best be getting home," he said:
    "The nights are very damp!"

He thought he saw a Garden-Door
  That opened with a key:
He looked again, and found it was
  A Double Rule of Three:
"And all its mystery," he said,
  "Is clear as day to me!"

He thought he saw an Argument
  That proved he was the Pope:
He looked again, and found it was
  A Bar of Mottled Soap.
"A fact so dread," he faintly said,
  "Extinguishes all hope!"

There be three Badgers on a mossy stone,
   Beside a dark and covered way:
Each dreams himself a monarch on his throne,
      And so they stay and stay—
Though their old Father languishes alone,
     They stay, and stay, and stay.

There be three Herrings loitering around,
   Longing to share that mossy seat:
Each Herring tries to sing what she has found
      That makes Life seem so sweet.
Thus, with a grating and uncertain sound,
     They bleat, and bleat, and bleat.

The Mother-Herring, on the salt sea-wave,
   Sought vainly for her absent ones:
The Father-Badger, writhing in a cave,
      Shrieked out "Return, my sons!
You shall have buns," he shrieked, "if you'll behave!
     Yea, buns, and buns, and buns!"

"I fear," said she, "your sons have gone astray?
    My daughters left me while I slept."
"Yes'm," the Badger said: "it's as you say."
        "They should be better kept."
Thus the poor parents talked the time away,
        And wept, and wept, and wept.

Oh, dear beyond our dearest dreams,
Fairer than all that fairest seems!
To feast the rosy hours away,
To revel in a roundelay!
        How blest would be
        A life so free—
Ipwergis-Pudding to consume,
And drink the subtle Azzigoom!

And if, in other days and hours,
Mid other fluffs and other flowers,
The choice were given me how to dine—

"Name what thou wilt: it shall be thine!"
        Oh, then I see
        The life for me—
Ipwergis-Pudding to consume,
And drink the subtle Azzigoom!

The Badgers did not care to talk to Fish:
    They did not dote on Herrings' songs:
They never had experienced the dish
        To which that name belongs:
"And oh, to pinch their tails," (this was their wish,)
        "With tongs, yea, tongs, and tongs!"

"And are not these the Fish," the Eldest sighed,
    "Whose Mother dwells beneath the foam?"
"They are the Fish!" the Second one replied.
        "And they have left their home!"
"Oh wicked Fish," the Youngest Badger cried,
        "To roam, yea, roam, and roam!"

Gently the Badgers trotted to the shore—
    The sandy shore that fringed the bay:
Each in his mouth a living Herring bore—
        Those aged ones waxed gay:
Clear rang their voices through the ocean's roar,
        "Hooray, hooray, hooray!"

He stept so lightly to the land,
    All in his manly pride:
He kissed her cheek, he pressed her hand,
    Yet still she glanced aside.
"Too gay he seems," she darkly dreams,
    "Too gallant and too gay
To think of me—poor simple me—
    When he is far away!"

"I bring my Love this goodly pearl
    Across the seas," he said:
"A gem to deck the dearest girl
    That ever sailor wed!"
She clasps it tight: her eyes are bright:
    Her throbbing heart would say
"He thought of me—he thought of me—
    When he was far away!"

The ship has sailed into the West:
    Her ocean-bird is flown:
A dull dead pain is in her breast,
    And she is weak and lone:
Yet there's a smile upon her face,
    A smile that seems to say
"He'll think of me—he'll think of me—
    When he is far away!

"Though waters wide between us glide,
    Our lives are warm and near:
No distance parts two faithful hearts—
    Two hearts that love so dear:
And I will trust my sailor-lad,
    For ever and a day,
To think of me—to think of me—
    When he is far away!"

from
Sylvie and Bruno Concluded

King Fisher courted Lady Bird—
Sing Beans, sing Bones, sing Butterflies!
   "Find me my match," he said,
   "With such a noble head—
With such a beard, as white as curd—
   With such expressive eyes!"

"Yet pins have heads," said Lady Bird—
Sing Prunes, sing Prawns, sing Primrose-Hill!
   "And, where you stick them in,
   They stay, and thus a pin
Is very much to be preferred
   To one that's never still!"

"Oysters have beards," said Lady Bird—
Sing Flies, sing Frogs, sing Fiddle-strings!
   "I love them, for I know
   They never chatter so:
They would not say one single word—
   Not if you crowned them Kings!"

"Needles have eyes," said Lady Bird—
Sing Cats, sing Corks, sing Cowslip-tea!
   "And they are sharp—just what
   Your Majesty is *not*:
So get you gone—'tis too absurd
   To come a-courting *me!*"

WHAT TOTTLES MEANT

"One thousand pounds per annum
Is not so bad a figure, come!"
Cried Tottles. "And I tell you, flat,
A man may marry well on that!
To say 'the Husband needs the Wife'
Is *not* the way to represent it.
The crowning joy of Woman's life
Is *Man!*" said Tottles (and he meant it).

The blissful Honey-moon is past:
The Pair have settled down at last:
Mamma-in-law their home will share,
And make their happiness her care.
"Your income is an ample one:
Go it, my children!" (and they went it).
"I *rayther* think this kind of fun
Won't last!" said Tottles (and he meant it).

They took a little country-box—
A box at Covent Garden also:
They lived a life of double-knocks,
Acquaintances began to call so:
Their London house was much the same
(It took three hundred, clear, to rent it):
"Life is a very jolly game!"
Cried happy Tottles (and he meant it).

"Contented with a frugal lot"
(He always used that phrase at Gunter's),
He bought a handy little yacht—
A dozen serviceable hunters—

The fishing of a Highland Loch—
A sailing-boat to circumvent it—
"The sounding of that Gaelic 'och'
Beats *me!*" said Tottles (and he meant it).

But oh, the worst of human ills
(Poor Tottles found) are "little bills"!
And, with no balance in the Bank,
What wonder that his spirits sank?
Still, as the money flowed away,
He wondered how on earth she spent it.
"You cost me twenty pounds a day,
At least!" cried Tottles (and he meant it).

She sighed. "Those Drawing Rooms, you know!
I really never thought about it:
Mamma declared we ought to go—
We should be Nobodies without it.
That diamond-circlet for my brow—
I quite believed that *she* had sent it,
Until the Bill came in just now—"
"*Viper!*" cried Tottles (and he meant it).

Poor Mrs. T. could bear no more,
But fainted flat upon the floor.
Mamma-in-law, with anguish wild,
Seeks, all in vain, to rouse her child.
"Quick! Take this box of smelling-salts!
Don't scold her, James, or you'll repent it,
She's a *dear* girl, with all her faults—"
"She *is!*" groaned Tottles (and he meant it).

"I was a donkey," Tottles cried,
"To choose your daughter for my bride!

'Twas *you* that bid us cut a dash!
'Tis *you* have brought us to this smash!
You don't suggest one single thing
That can in any way prevent it—
Then what's the use of arguing?
Shut up!" cried Tottles (and he meant it).

"And now the mischief's done, perhaps
You'll kindly go and pack your traps?
Since *two* (your daughter and your son)
Are Company, but *three* are none.
A course of saving we'll begin:
When change is needed, I'll invent it:
Don't think to put *your* finger in
This pie!" cried Tottles (and he meant it).

See now this couple settled down
In quiet lodgings, out of town:
Submissively the tearful wife
Accepts a plain and humble life:
Yet begs one boon on bended knee:
"My ducky-darling, don't resent it!
Mamma might come for two or three—"
"*NEVER!*" yelled Tottles. And he meant it.

In stature the Manlet was dwarfish—
    No burly big Blunderbore he:
And he wearily gazed on the crawfish
    His Wifelet had dressed for his tea.
"Now reach me, sweet Atom, my gunlet
    And hurl the old shoelet for luck:
Let me hie to the bank of the runlet,
            And shoot thee a Duck!"

She has reached him his minikin gunlet:
    She has hurled the old shoelet for luck:
She is busily baking a bunlet,
    To welcome him home with his Duck.
On he speeds, never wasting a wordlet,
    Though thoughtlets cling, closely as wax,
To the spot where the beautiful birdlet
            So quietly quacks.

Where the Lobsterlet lurks, and the Crablet
    So slowly and sleepily crawls:
Where the Dolphin's at home, and the Dablet
    Pays long ceremonious calls:
Where the Grublet is sought by the Froglet:
    Where the Frog is pursued by the Duck:
Where the Ducklet is chased by the Doglet—
            So runs the world's luck!

He has loaded with bullet and powder:
    His footfall is noiseless as air:
But the Voices grow louder and louder,
    And bellow, and bluster, and blare.
They bristle before him and after,
    They flutter above and below,
Shrill shriekings of lubberly laughter,
            Weird wailings of woe!

They echo without him, within him:
  They thrill through his whiskers and beard:
Like a teetotum seeming to spin him,
  With sneers never hitherto sneered.
"Avengement," they cry, "on our Foelet!
  Let the Manikin weep for our wrongs!
Let us drench him, from toplet to toelet,
        With Nursery-Songs!

"He shall muse upon 'Hey! Diddle! Diddle!'
  On the Cow that surmounted the Moon:
He shall rave of the Cat and the Fiddle,
  And the Dish that eloped with the Spoon:
And his soul shall be sad for the Spider,
  When Miss Muffet was sipping her whey,
That so tenderly sat down beside her,
        And scared her away!

"The music of Midsummer-madness
    Shall sting him with many a bite,
Till, in rapture of rollicking sadness,
    He shall groan with a gloomy delight:
He shall swathe him, like mists of the morning,
    In platitudes luscious and limp,
Such as deck, with a deathless adorning,
            The Song of the Shrimp!

"When the Ducklet's dark doom is decided,
    We will trundle him home in a trice:
And the banquet, so plainly provided,
    Shall round into rose-buds and rice:
In a blaze of pragmatic invention
    He shall wrestle with Fate, and shall reign:
But he has not a friend fit to mention,
            So hit him again!"

He has shot it, the delicate darling!
    And the Voices have ceased from their strife:
Not a whisper of sneering or snarling,
    As he carries it home to his wife:
Then, cheerily champing the bunlet
    His spouse was so skilful to bake,
He hies him once more to the runlet,
            To fetch her the Drake!

THE PIG-TALE

Introductory Verses

Little Birds are dining
  Warily and well,
  Hid in mossy cell:
Hid, I say, by waiters
  Gorgeous in their gaiters—
  I've a Tale to tell.

Little Birds are feeding
  Justices with jam,
  Rich in frizzled ham:
Rich, I say, in oysters
  Haunting shady cloisters—
  That is what I am.

Little Birds are teaching
  Tigresses to smile,
  Innocent of guile:
Smile, I say, not smirkle—
  Mouth a semicircle,
  That's the proper style!

Little Birds are sleeping
  All among the pins,
  Where the loser wins:
Where, I say, he sneezes
  When and how he pleases—
  So the Tale begins.

There was a Pig that sat alone
    Beside a ruined Pump:
By day and night he made his moan—
It would have stirred a heart of stone
To see him wring his hoofs and groan,
    Because he could not jump.

A certain Camel heard him shout—
    A Camel with a hump.
"Oh, is it Grief, or is it Gout?
What is this bellowing about?"
That Pig replied, with quivering snout,
    "Because I cannot jump!"

That Camel scanned him, dreamy-eyed.
    "Methinks you are too plump.
I never knew a Pig so wide—
That wobbled so from side to side—
Who could, however much he tried,
    Do such a thing as *jump!*

"Yet mark those trees, two miles away,
    All clustered in a clump;
If you could trot there twice a day,
Nor ever pause for rest or play,
In the far future—Who can say?—
    You may be fit to jump."

That Camel passed, and left him there
    Beside the ruined Pump.
Oh, horrid was that Pig's despair!
His shrieks of anguish filled the air.
He wrung his hoofs, he rent his hair,
    Because he could not jump.

There was a Frog that wandered by—
    A sleek and shining lump:
Inspected him with fishy eye,
And said "O Pig, what makes you cry?"
And bitter was that Pig's reply,
    "Because I cannot jump!"

That Frog he grinned a grin of glee,
    And hit his chest a thump.
"O Pig," he said, "be ruled by me,
And you shall see what you shall see.
This minute, for a trifling fee,
    I'll teach you how to jump!

"You may be faint from many a fall,
    And bruised by many a bump:
But, if you persevere through all,
And practise first on something small,
Concluding with a ten-foot wall,
    You'll find that you *can* jump!"

That Pig looked up with joyful start:
    "Oh Frog, you are a trump!
Your words have healed my inward smart—
Come, name your fee and do your part:
Bring comfort to a broken heart,
    By teaching me to jump!"

"My fee shall be a mutton chop,
    My goal this ruined Pump.
Observe with what an airy flop
I plant myself upon the top!
Now bend your knees and take a hop,
    For that's the way to jump!"

Uprose that Pig, and rushed, full whack,
    Against the ruined Pump:
Rolled over like an empty sack,
And settled down upon his back,
While all his bones at once went 'Crack!'
    It was a fatal jump.

Little Birds are writing
    Interesting books,
        To be read by cooks:
Read, I say, not roasted—
Letterpress, when toasted,
    Loses its good looks.

Little birds are playing
    Bagpipes on the shore,
        Where the tourists snore:

"Thanks!" they cry. " 'Tis thrilling!
Take, oh take this shilling!
    Let us have no more!"

Little birds are bathing
    Crocodiles in cream,
    Like a happy dream:
Like, but not so lasting—
Crocodiles, when fasting,
    Are not all they seem!

That Camel passed, as Day grew dim
    Around the ruined Pump.
"O broken heart! O broken limb!
It needs," that Camel said to him,
"Something more fairy-like and slim,
    To execute a jump!"

That Pig lay still as any stone,
     And could not stir a stump:
Nor ever, if the truth were known,
Was he again observed to moan,
Nor ever wring his hoofs and groan,
     Because he could not jump.

That Frog made no remark, for he
     Was dismal as a dump:
He knew the consequence must be
That he would never get his fee—
And still he sits, in miserie,
     Upon that ruined Pump!

Little Birds are choking
     Baronets with bun,
          Taught to fire a gun:
     Taught, I say, to splinter
     Salmon in the winter—
          Merely for the fun.

Little Birds are hiding
    Crimes in carpet bags,
    Blessed by happy stags:
Blessed, I say, though beaten—
Since our friends are eaten
    When the memory flags.

Little Birds are tasting
    Gratitude and gold,
    Pale with sudden cold:
Pale, I say, and wrinkled—
When the bells have tinkled,
    And the Tale is told.

More Parodies

and
Other
Humorous
Verse

HIAWATHA'S PHOTOGRAPHING

[INTRODUCTION BY THE AUTHOR.—*In these days of imitation I can claim no sort of merit for this slight attempt at doing what is known to be so easy. Any one that knows what verse is, with the smallest ear for rhythm, can throw off a composition in an easy, running metre like "The Song of Hiawatha." Having, then, distinctly stated that I challenge no attention in the following little poem to its merely verbal jingle, I must beg the candid reader to confine his criticism to its treatment of the subject.*]

From his shoulder Hiawatha
Took the camera of rosewood—
Made of sliding, folding rosewood—
Neatly put it all together.
In its case it lay compactly,
Folded into nearly nothing;
But he opened out the hinges,
Pushed and pulled the joints and hinges,
Till it looked all squares and oblongs,
Like a complicated figure
In the Second Book of Euclid.
This he perched upon a tripod,
And the family, in order,

Sat before him for their pictures—
Mystic, awful, was the process.

    First, a piece of glass he coated
With collodion, and plunged it
In a bath of lunar caustic
Carefully dissolved in water—
There he left it certain minutes.

    Secondly, my Hiawatha
Made with cunning hand a mixture
Of the acid pyrro-gallic,
And of glacial-acetic,
And of alcohol and water—
This developed all the picture.

    Finally he fixed each picture
With a saturate solution
Which was made of hyposulphite,
Which, again, was made of soda.
(Very difficult the name is
For a metre like the present,
But periphrasis has done it.)

    All the family in order,
Sat before him for their pictures;
Each in turn, as he was taken,
Volunteered his own suggestions—
His invaluable suggestions.

    First, the governor—the father—
He suggested velvet curtains
Looped about a massy pillar,
And the corner of a table—
Of a rosewood dining-table—
He would hold a scroll of something—
Hold it firmly in his left-hand;
He would keep his right-hand buried
(Like Napoleon) in his waistcoat;

He would gaze upon the distance—
(Like a poet seeing visions,
Like a man that plots a poem,
In a dressing-gown of damask,
At 12:30 in the morning,

Ere the servants bring in luncheon)—
With a look of pensive meaning,
As of ducks that die in tempests.
  Grand, heroic was the notion:
Yet the picture failed entirely,
Failed because he moved a little—
Moved because he couldn't help it.
  Next his better half took courage—
She would have her picture taken:
She came dressed beyond description,
Dressed in jewels and in satin,
Far too gorgeous for an empress.
Gracefully she sat down sideways,
With a simper scarcely human,
Holding in her hand a nosegay
Rather larger than a cabbage.
All the while that she was taking,
Still the lady chattered, chattered,
Like a monkey in the forest.
"Am I sitting still?" she asked him;
"Is my face enough in profile?
Shall I hold the nosegay higher?
Will it come into the picture?"
And the picture failed completely.
  Next the son, the stunning Cantab,
He suggested curves of beauty,
Curves pervading all his figure,
Which the eye might follow onward
Till they centered in the breast-pin—
Centered in the golden breast-pin.
He had learnt it all from Ruskin,
(Author of "The Stones of Venice,"
"Seven Lamps of Architecture,"
"Modern Painters," and some others)—

And perhaps he had not fully
Understood his author's meaning;
But, whatever was the reason,
All was fruitless, as the picture
Ended in a total failure.

After him the eldest daughter:
She suggested very little,
Only begged she might be taken
With her look of "passive beauty."
Her idea of passive beauty

Was a squinting of the left-eye,
Was a drooping of the right-eye,
Was a smile that went up sideways
To the corner of the nostrils.

Hiawatha, when she asked him,
Took no notice of the question,
Looked as if he hadn't heard it;
But, when pointedly appealed to,
Smiled in a peculiar manner,
Coughed, and said it "didn't matter,"
Bit his lips, and changed the subject.

Nor in this was he mistaken,
As the picture failed completely.

So, in turn, the other daughters:
All of them agreed in one thing,
That their pictures came to nothing,
Though they differed in their causes,
From the eldest, Grinny-haha,
Who, throughout her time of taking,
Shook with sudden, causeless laughter,
With a fit of silent laughter,
To the youngest, Dinny-wawa,
Who, throughout her time of taking,
Shook with sudden, causeless weeping—
Anything but silent weeping;
And their pictures failed completely.
Last, the youngest son was taken:
"John" his Christian name had once been;
But his overbearing sisters
Called him names he disapproved of—
Called him Johnny, "Daddy's Darling"—
Called him Jacky, "Scrubby Schoolboy."
Very rough and thick his hair was,
Very round and red his face was,
Very dusty was his jacket,

Very fidgetty his manner,
And, so fearful was the picture,
In comparison the others
Might be thought to have succeeded—
To have partially succeeded.
　　Finally, my Hiawatha
Tumbled all the tribe together

("Grouped" is not the right expression),
And, as happy chance would have it,
Did at last obtain a picture
Where the faces all succeeded:
Each came out a perfect likeness.

   Then they joined and all abused it—
Unrestrainedly abused it—
As "the worst and ugliest picture
That could possibly be taken.
Giving one such strange expressions!
Sulkiness, conceit and meanness!
Really any one would take us
(Any one that did not know us)
For the most unpleasant people!"
(Hiawatha seemed to think so—
Seemed to think it not unlikely.)
All together rang their voices—
Angry, loud, discordant voices—
As of dogs that howl in concert,
As of cats that wail in chorus.

   But my Hiawatha's patience,
His politeness, and his manners,
Unaccountably had vanished.
Not a minute more he waited,
But, to use his own expression,
His American expression,
Packed his traps, and "sloped for Texas."
Neither did he leave them slowly,
With that calm deliberation—
Which photographers aspire to,
But he left them in a hurry—
Left them in a mighty passion—
Stating that he would not stand it,
Stating, in emphatic language,
What he'd be before he'd stand it.

from "THE LEGEND OF SCOTLAND"

Lorenzo dwelt at Heighington,
   (Hys cote was made of Dimity,)
Least-ways yf not exactly there,
   Yet yn yts close proximity.
Hee called on mee—hee stayed to tee—
   Yet not a word he ut-tered,
Untyl I sayd, "D'ye lyke your bread
   Dry?" and hee answered "But-tered."

    Chorus

   Noodle dumb
   Has a noodle-head,
I hate such noodles, *I* do.

A SEA-DIRGE

There are certain things—as, a spider, a ghost,
   The income-tax, gout, an umbrella for three—
That I hate, but the thing that I hate the most
   Is a thing they call the Sea.

Pour some salt water on to the floor—
   Ugly I'm sure you'll confess it to be:—
Suppose it extended a mile or more,
   That's very like the Sea.

Pinch a dog till it howls outright—
   Cruel, but all very well for a spree;—
Suppose that it did so day and night,
   That would be like the Sea.

I had a vision of nursery-maids,
   Tens of thousands passed by me,
All leading children and wooden spades,
   And this was by the Sea.

Who invented those spades of wood?
   Who was it cut them out of the tree?
None, I think, but an idiot could,
   Or one that loved the Sea.

It is pleasant and dreamy, no doubt, to float
   With "thoughts as boundless, and souls as free"—
But suppose you are very unwell in the boat,
   How do you like the Sea?

"But it makes the intellect clear and keen"—
   "Prove it! prove it! how can that be?
"Why, what does 'B sharp,' (in music) mean,
   "If not 'the natural C'?"

What! keen? with such questions as "when's high tide?
   "Is shelling shrimps an improvement to tea?
"Were donkeys intended for Man to ride?"
   Such are our thoughts by the Sea.

There is an insect that people avoid,
   (Whence is derived the verb 'to flee,')
Where have you been by it most annoyed?
   In lodgings by the Sea.

If you like coffee with sand for dregs,
   A decided hint of salt in your tea,
And a fishy taste in the very eggs—
   By all means choose the Sea.

And if, with these dainties to drink and to eat,
    You prefer not a vestige of grass or tree,
And a chronic state of wet in your feet,
    Then—I recommend the Sea.

For *I* have friends who dwell by the coast,
    Pleasant friends they are to me:
It is when I am with them I wonder most
    That any one likes the Sea.

They take me a walk; though tired and stiff,
    To climb the heights I madly agree:
And, after a tumble or so from the cliff,
    They kindly suggest the Sea.

I try the rocks; and I think it cool
    That they laugh with such an excess of glee,
As I heavily slip into every pool
    That skirts the cold, cold Sea.

Once I met a friend in the street,
    With wife, and nurse, and children three:
Never again such a sight may I meet
    As that party from the Sea.

Their cheeks were hollow, their steps were slow,
    Convicted felons they seemed to be:
"Are you going to prison, dear friend?" "Oh no!
    "We're returning—from the Sea!"

DISILLUSIONISED

I painted her a gushing thing—
    Her years perhaps a score;
I little thought to find them
    At least two dozen more!
My fancy gave her eyes of blue,
    A curling auburn head;
I came to find the blue a green,
    The auburn grown to red!

I painted her a lip and cheek
    In colour like the rose;
I little thought the selfsame hue
    Extended to her nose!
I dreamed of rounded features—
    A smile of ready glee—
But it was not *fat* I wanted,
    Nor a *grin* I hoped to see!

She boxed my ears this morning—
    They tingled very much—
I own that I could wish her
    A somewhat lighter touch:
And if I were to settle how
    Her charms might be improved,
I would not have them added to,
    But just a few removed!

She has the bear's ethereal grace,
    The bland hyena's laugh,
The footstep of the elephant,
    The neck of the giraffe:

I love her still—believe it—
  Though my heart its passion hides;
She's all my fancy painted her,
  But oh! how much besides!

YE CARPETTE KNYGHTE

I have a horse—a ryghte goode horse—
  Ne doe I envye those
Who scoure ye playne yn headye course
  Tyll soddayne on theyre nose
They lyghte wyth unexpected force—
  Yt ys—a horse of clothes.

I have a saddel—"Say'st thou soe?
  Wyth styrruppes, Knyghte, to boote?"
I sayde not that—I answere "Noe"—
  Yt lacketh such, I woote:
Yt ys a mutton-saddel, loe!
  Parte of ye fleecye brute.

I have a bytte—a ryghte good bytte—
  As shall bee seene yn tyme.
Ye jawe of horse yt wyll not fytte;
  Yts use ys more sublyme.
Fayre Syr, how deemest thou of yt?
  Yt ys—thys bytte of rhyme.

POETA FIT, NON NASCITUR

"How shall I be a poet?
    How shall I write in rhyme?
You told me once 'the very wish
    Partook of the sublime.'
Then tell me how! Don't put me off
    With your 'another time'!"

The old man smiled to see him,
    To hear his sudden sally;
He liked the lad to speak his mind
    Enthusiastically;
And thought "There's no hum-drum in him,
    Nor any shilly-shally."

"And would you be a poet
    Before you've been to school?
Ah, well! I hardly thought you
    So absolute a fool.
First learn to be spasmodic—
    A very simple rule.

"For first you write a sentence,
    And then you chop it small;
Then mix the bits, and sort them out
    Just as they chance to fall:
The order of the phrases makes
    No difference at all.

"Then, if you'd be impressive,
    Remember what I say,
That abstract qualities begin
    With capitals alway:
The True, the Good, the Beautiful—
    Those are the things that pay!

"Next, when you are describing
    A shape, or sound, or tint;
Don't state the matter plainly,
    But put it in a hint;
And learn to look at all things
    With a sort of mental squint."

"For instance, if I wished, Sir,
    Of mutton-pies to tell,
Should I say 'dreams of fleecy flocks
    Pent in a wheaten cell'?"
"Why, yes," the old man said: "that phrase
    Would answer very well.

"Then fourthly, there are epithets
    That suit with any word—
As well as Harvey's Reading Sauce
    With fish or flesh, or bird—
Of these 'wild,' 'lonely,' 'weary,' 'strange,'
    Are much to be preferred."

"And will it do, O will it do
    To take them in a lump—
As 'the wild man went his weary way
    To a strange and lonely pump'?"
"Nay, nay! You must not hastily
    To such conclusions jump.

"Such epithets, like pepper,
    Give zest to what you write;
And, if you strew them sparely,
    They whet the appetite:
But if you lay them on too thick,
    You spoil the matter quite!

"Last, as to the arrangement:
    Your reader, you should show him,
Must take what information he
    Can get, and look for no im-
mature disclosure of the drift
    And purpose of your poem.

"Therefore, to test his patience—
    How much he can endure—
Mention no places, names, or dates,
    And evermore be sure
Throughout the poem to be found
    Consistently obscure.

"First fix upon the limit
    To which it shall extend:
Then fill it up with 'Padding'
    (Beg some of any friend):
Your great SENSATION-STANZA
    You place towards the end."

"And what is a Sensation,
    Grandfather, tell me, pray?
I think I never heard the word
    So used before to-day:
Be kind enough to mention one
    'Exempli gratia.'"

And the old man, looking sadly
    Across the garden-lawn,
Where here and there a dew-drop
    Yet glittered in the dawn,
Said "Go to the Adelphi,
    And see the 'Colleen Bawn.'

"The word is due to Boucicault—
    The theory is his,
Where Life becomes a Spasm,
    And History a Whiz:
If that is not Sensation,
    I don't know what it is.

"Now try your hand, ere Fancy
    Have lost its present glow—"
"And then," his grandson added,
    "We'll publish it, you know:
Green cloth—gold-lettered at the back—
    In duodecimo!"

Then proudly smiled that old man
  To see the eager lad
Rush madly for his pen and ink
  And for his blotting-pad—
But, when he thought of *publishing,*
  His face grew stern and sad.

Puzzles,
Acrostics,
Dedications,

and Riddles

All in the golden afternoon
　　Full leisurely we glide;
For both our oars, with little skill,
　　By little arms are plied,
While little hands make vain pretence
　　Our wanderings to guide.

Ah, cruel Three! In such an hour,
　　Beneath such dreamy weather,
To beg a tale of breath too weak
　　To stir the tiniest feather!
Yet what can one poor voice avail
　　Against three tongues together?

Imperious Prima flashes forth
　　Her edict "to begin it":
In gentler tones Secunda hopes
　　"There will be nonsense in it."
While Tertia interrupts the tale
　　Not *more* than once a minute.

Anon, to sudden silence won,
　　In fancy they pursue
The dream-child moving through a land
　　Of wonders wild and new,
In friendly chat with bird or beast—
　　And half believe it true.

And ever, as the story drained
　　The wells of fancy dry,
And faintly strove that weary one
　　To put the subject by,
"The rest next time—" "It *is* next time!"
　　The happy voices cry.

Thus grew the tale of Wonderland:
    Thus slowly, one by one,
Its quaint events were hammered out—
    And now the tale is done,
And home we steer, a merry crew,
    Beneath the setting sun.

Alice! A childish story take,
    And with a gentle hand
Lay it where Childhood's dreams are twined
    In Memory's mystic band,
Like pilgrim's withered wreath of flowers
    Plucked in a far-off land.

Child of the pure unclouded brow
  And dreaming eyes of wonder!
Though time be fleet, and I and thou
  Are half a life asunder,
Thy loving smile will surely hail
The love-gift of a fairy-tale.

I have not seen thy sunny face,
  Nor heard thy silver laughter:
No thought of me shall find a place
  In thy young life's hereafter—
Enough that now thou wilt not fail
To listen to my fairy-tale.

A tale begun in other days,
  When summer suns were glowing—
A simple chime, that served to time
  The rhythm of our rowing—
Whose echoes live in memory yet,
Though envious years would say 'forget.'

Come, harken then, ere voice of dread,
  With bitter tidings laden,
Shall summon to unwelcome bed
  A melancholy maiden!
We are but older children, dear,
Who fret to find our bedtime near.

Without, the frost, the blinding snow,
  The storm-wind's moody madness—
Within, the firelight's ruddy glow,
  And childhood's nest of gladness.
The magic words shall hold thee fast:
Thou shalt not heed the raving blast.

And, though the shadow of a sigh
  May tremble through the story,
For 'happy summer days' gone by,
  And vanish'd summer glory—
It shall not touch, with breath of bale,
  The pleasance of our fairy-tale.

A boat, beneath a sunny sky
Lingering onward dreamily
In an evening of July—

Children three that nestle near,
Eager eye and willing ear,
Pleased a simple tale to hear—

Long has paled that sunny sky:
Echoes fade and memories die:
Autumn frosts have slain July.

Still she haunts me, phantomwise,
Alice moving under skies
Never seen by waking eyes.

Children yet, the tale to hear,
Eager eye and willing ear,
Lovingly shall nestle near.

In a Wonderland they lie,
Dreaming as the days go by,
Dreaming as the summers die:

Ever drifting down the stream—
Lingering in the golden gleam—
Life, what is it but a dream?

*An acrostic poem. The first letters of each line spell the name of
Alice Pleasance Liddell.*

Inscribed to a dear Child:
in memory of golden summer hours
and whispers of a summer sea.

Girt with a boyish garb for boyish task,
　　Eager she wields her spade: yet loves as well
Rest on a friendly knee, intent to ask
　　　　The tale he loves to tell.

Rude spirits of the seething outer strife,
　　Unmeet to read her pure and simple spright,
Deem, if you list, such hours a waste of life,
　　　　Empty of all delight!

Chat on, sweet Maid, and rescue from annoy
　　Hearts that by wiser talk are unbeguiled.
Ah, happy he who owns that tenderest joy,
　　　　The heart-love of a child!

Away, fond thoughts, and vex my soul no more!
　　Work claims my wakeful nights, my busy days—
Albeit bright memories of that sunlit shore
　　　　Yet haunt my dreaming gaze!

⁓⁓

A double acrostic. The first letters of each line, and also the first
words of each stanza, spell out the name Gertrude Chataway.

Is all our Life, then, but a dream
Seen faintly in the golden gleam
Athwart Time's dark resistless stream?

Bowed to the earth with bitter woe
Or laughing at some raree-show,
We flutter idly to and fro.

Man's little Day in haste we spend,
And, from its merry noontide, send
No glance to meet the silent end.

A double acrostic. The name Isa Bowman is spelled out by the first letters of each line, and by the first three letters of each stanza.

"Jgmu qjl vgrv x ugemdt pupdeto?" wxxl x ugmh vj
    f jji.
"Ge'n ijsk tukcbb qfds fb qrug eq xud eyk cxdmfit
    ddjdef:
Fbu cgkskg mglb gf mstutt, had ubj. okc Ljudz *jgmu*
    nt jxxmh,
Pa st'ok krv eykgb vj dogoq grukc vqb zmfvtn as
    tuemak exjmh."
Wrs-brs, brs-brs, wrs-brs, brs-brs: "Vrct fdjsi!"
    fgu, Ugmh.
Njj-sjj, sjj-sjj, njj-sjj, sjj-sjj; Jji wxxl "Urbe ek
    fxdmh."

"Ljsv efdn ma lb as zapsi hlgvv," wxxl Srr, "zru
    qrmxbr yadsl!
Lh jtbv xok urbt jgey zxmkkm imlk, eyce nypdef mhtt
    vj mht zxjlbu.
Xv pn dz rsk xbcbbexak—na Urdmh btblk'm wvrdu:
Nht dok'm gkkkm o ifvtsu ruut mhkm'w brxey
    genstxiqmgk zamc!"
Njj-sjj, sjj-sjj, njj-sjj, sjj-sjj: "G urbe dogb jjo
    Ljudz!"
Eab-jab, jab-jab, eab-jab, jab-jab: Umgh wxxl
    "Eyoe'n jjudz."

[TRANSLATION OF THE CIPHER]

[Note.—*Lily and Fox were two Dogs.*]

"Will you trot a little quicker?" said a Lily to a Fox.
"It's gone eleven half an hour, by all the village clocks:
And dinner-time is twelve, you know, and Dolly *will* be wrath,
If we're not there to carry round the plates of mutton-broth."
Bow-wow, bow-wow, bow-wow, bow-wow: "Come along!" said
    Lily.
Bow-wow, bow-wow, bow-wow, bow-wow: Fox said "Don't be
    silly."

"Don't talk to me of going quick," said Fox, "you howling
    Hound!
My feet are done with patent glue, that sticks them to the
    ground.
It is my own invention—so Dolly needn't scold:
She can't invent a patent glue that's worth its weight in gold!"
Bow-wow, bow-wow, bow-wow, bow-wow: "*I* don't carry for
    Dolly!"
Bow-wow, bow-wow, bow-wow, bow-wow; Lily said "that's
    folly."

[PUZZLE]

(To Mary, Ina, and Harriet or "Hartie" Watson.)

When .a.y and I.a told .a..ie they'd seen a
   Small ..ea.u.e with .i..., dressed in crimson and
     blue,
.a..ie cried " 'Twas a .ai.y! Why, I.a and .a.y,
   I *should* have been happy if I had been you!"

Said .a.y "You wouldn't." Said I.a "You shouldn't—
   Since *you* can't be *us,* and *we* couldn't be *you.*
You are *one,* my dear .a..ie, but *we* are a .a..y,
   And a.i...e.i. tells us that *one* isn't *two.*"

*Although the editor has never seen the answer in print, the missing
words would seem to be: Mary, Ina, Hartie, creature, wings, Hartie,
fairy, Ina, Mary, Mary, Ina, Hartie, party, arithmetic!*

PUZZLES FROM WONDERLAND

I.

Dreaming of apples on a wall,
   And dreaming often, dear,
I dreamed that if I counted all,
   How many would appear?

II.

A stick I found, that weighed two pound:
   I sawed it up one day
In pieces eight, of equal weight.
   How much did each piece weigh?

[Everybody says "a quarter of a pound," which is wrong.]

III.

John gave his brother James a box:
About it there were many locks.

James woke, and said it gave him pain;
So gave it back to John again.

This box was not with lid supplied,
Yet caused two lids to open wide:

And all these locks had never a key—
What kind of box, then, could it be?

IV.

What is most like a bee in May?
"Well, let me think: perhaps—" you say.
Bravo! You're guessing well to-day!

V.

Three sisters at breakfast were feeding the cat.
The first gave it sole—Puss was grateful for that:
The next gave it salmon—which Puss thought a treat:
The third gave it herring—which Puss wouldn't eat.

[*Explain the conduct of the cat.*]

VI.

Said the Moon to the Sun,
  "Is the daylight begun?"
Said the Sun to the Moon,
  "Not a minute too soon."

"You're a Full Moon," said he.
  She replied with a frown,
"Well! I never *did* see
  So uncivil a clown!"

[Query. *Why was the moon so angry?*]

VII.

When the King found that his money was nearly all gone,
and that he really *must* live more economically, he decided on
sending away most of his Wise Men. There were some hundreds
of them—very fine old men, and magnificently dressed in green
velvet gowns with gold buttons: if they *had* a fault, it was that
they always contradicted one another when he asked for their
advice—and they certainly ate and drank *enormously*. So, on the
whole, he was rather glad to get rid of them. But there was an
old law, which he did not dare to disobey, which said that there
must always be

"Seven blind of both eyes:
  Ten blind of one eye:

Five that see with both eyes:
  Nine that see with one eye."

[Query. *How many did he keep?*]

SOLUTIONS TO PUZZLES FROM
WONDERLAND

I.   If ten the number dreamed of, why 'tis clear
     That in the dream ten apples would appear.

II. In Shylock's bargain for the flesh, was found
     No mention of the blood that flowed around;
     So when the stick was sawed in pieces eight,
     The sawdust lost diminished from the weight.

III. As curly-wigg'd Jemmy was sleeping in bed
     His brother John gave him a blow on the head;
     James opened his eyelids, and spying his brother,
     Doubled his fist, and gave him another.
     This kind of box then is not so rare;
     The lids are the eyelids, the locks are the hair;
     And as every schoolboy can tell to his cost,
     The key to the tangles is constantly lost.

IV.   'Twixt "Perhaps" and "May be"
      Little difference we see:
      Let the question go round,
      The answer is found.

V.   That salmon and sole Puss should think very grand
      Is no such remarkable thing,
      For more of these dainties Puss took up her stand:
      But when the third sister stretched out her fair hand
      Pray why should Puss swallow her ring?

VI.   "In these degenerate days," we oft hear said,
      "Manners are lost, and chivalry is dead!"
      No wonder, since in high exalted spheres
      The same degeneracy, in fact, appears.

      The Moon in social matters interfering,
      Scolded the Sun, when early in appearing;
      And the rude Sun, her gentle sex ignoring,
      Called her a fool, thus her pretensions flooring.

VII.   Five seeing, and seven blind,
      Give us twelve in all, we find;
      But all of these, 'tis very plain,
      Come into account again.
      For take notice, it may be true,
      That those blind of one eye are blind of two;
      And consider contrariwise,
      That to see with your eye you may have your eyes;
      So setting one against the other—
      For a mathematician no great bother—
      And working the sum, you will understand
      That sixteen wise men still trouble the land.

EADGYTH.

(*To Mabel and Emily Kerr*)

Thanks, thanks, fair Cousins, for your gift
  So swiftly borne to Albion's isle—
Though angry waves their crests uplift
  Between our shores for many a league!　　　　　MilE

("So far, so good," you say: "but how
  Your Cousins?" Let me tell you, Madam.
We're both descended, you'll allow,
  From one great-great-great grandsire, Noah.)　　AdaM

Your picture shall adorn the book
  That's bound so neatly and morroccoly,
With that bright green which every cook
  Delights to see in beds of cauliflower.　　　　BroccolI

The carte is very good, but pray
  Send me the larger one as well!
"A cool request!" I hear you say,
  "Give him an inch, he takes an acre!　　　　　ElL

"But we'll be generous, because
  We well remember, in the story,
How good and gentle Alice was,
  The day she argued with the Parrot!"　　　　　LorY

~~~~

*The first and last letters of the "riddle" words spell the names of
Mabel and Emily, and each word of the riddle rhymes with the last
word of the second line of its stanza.*

"Are you deaf, Father William?" the young man said.
"Did you hear what I told you just now?
"Excuse me for shouting! Don't waggle your head
"Like a blundering, sleepy old cow!
"A little maid dwelling in Wallington Town,
"Is my friend, so I beg to remark:
"Do you think she'd be pleased if a book were sent down
"Entitled 'The Hunt of the Snark?'"

"Pack it up in brown paper!" the old man cried,
"And seal it with olive-and-dove.
"I command you to do it!" he added with pride,
"Nor forget, my dear fellow, to send her beside
"Easter Greetings, and give her my love."

*An acrostic poem. The first letters of each line spell the name
Adelaide Paine.*

"Maidens! if you love the tale,
      If you love the Snark,
Need I urge you, spread the sail,
Now, while freshly blows the gale,
      In your ocean-barque!

"English Maidens love renown,
      Enterprise, and fuss!"
Laughingly those Maidens frown;
Laughingly, with eyes cast down;
      And they answer thus:

"English Maidens fear to roam.
      Much we dread the dark;
Much we dread what ills might come,
If we left our English home,
      Even for a Snark!"

The names Minnie, Ella and Emmie can be found by reading the first letters of each line.

The Hunting of the Snark:

An Agony in Eight Fits

Preface

If—and the thing is wildly possible—the charge of writing nonsense were ever brought against the author of this brief but instructive poem, it would be based, I feel convinced, on the line . . .

"Then the bowsprit got mixed with the rudder sometimes."

In view of this painful possibility, I will not (as I might) appeal indignantly to my other writings as a proof that I am incapable of such a deed: I will not (as I might) point to the strong moral purpose of this poem itself, to the arithmetical principles so cautiously inculcated in it, or to its noble teachings in Natural History—I will take the more prosaic course of simply explaining how it happened.

The Bellman, who was almost morbidly sensitive about appearances, used to have the bowsprit unshipped once or twice a week to be revarnished, and it more than once happened, when the time came for replacing it, that no one on board could remember which end of the ship it belonged to. They knew it was not of the slightest use to appeal to the Bellman about it —he would only refer to his Naval Code, and read out in pathetic tones Admiralty Instructions which none of them had ever been able to understand—so it generally ended in its being fastened on, anyhow, across the rudder. The helmsman* used to stand by with tears in his eyes: *he* knew it was all wrong, but alas! Rule 42 of the Code, *"No one shall speak to the Man at the Helm,"* had been completed by the Bellman himself with the words *"and the Man at the Helm shall speak to no one."* So remonstrance was impossible, and no steering could be done till the next varnishing day. During these bewildering intervals the ship usually sailed backwards.

As this poem is to some extent connected with the lay of the Jabberwock, let me take this opportunity of answering a question that has often been asked me, how to pronounce "slithy toves." The "i" in "slithy" is long, as in "write"; and "toves" is pronounced so as to rhyme with "groves." Again, the first "o" in "borogoves" is pronounced like the "o" in "borrow." I have heard people try to give it the sound of the "o" in worry. Such is Human Perversity.

This also seems a fitting occasion to notice the other hard words in that poem. Humpty-Dumpty's theory, of two meanings packed into one word like a portmanteau, seems to me the right explanation for all.

For instance, take the two words "fuming" and "furious." Make up your mind that you will say both words, but leave it unsettled which you will say first. Now open your mouth and speak. If your thoughts incline ever so little towards "fuming," you will say "fuming-furious;" if they turn, by even a hair's breadth, towards "furious," you will say "furious-fuming;" but if you have that rarest of gifts, a perfectly balanced mind, you will say "frumious."

---

* This office was usually undertaken by the Boots, who found in it a refuge from the Baker's constant complaints about the insufficient blacking of his three pair of boots.

Supposing that, when Pistol uttered the well-known words—

"Under which king, Bezonian? Speak or die!"

Justice Shallow had felt certain that it was either William or Richard, but had not been able to settle which, so that he could not possibly say either name before the other, can it be doubted that, rather than die, he would have gasped out "Rilchiam!"

THE HUNTING OF THE SNARK

Fit the First
The Landing

"Just the place for a Snark!" the Bellman cried,
  As he landed his crew with care;
Supporting each man on the top of the tide
  By a finger entwined in his hair.

"Just the place for a Snark! I have said it twice:
  That alone should encourage the crew.
Just the place for a Snark! I have said it thrice:
  What I tell you three times is true."

The crew was complete: it included a Boots—
  A maker of Bonnets and Hoods—
A Barrister, brought to arrange their disputes—
  And a Broker, to value their goods.

A Billiard-marker, whose skill was immense,
  Might perhaps have won more than his share—
But a Banker, engaged at enormous expense,
  Had the whole of their cash in his care.

There was also a Beaver, that paced on the deck,
    Or would sit making lace in the bow:
And had often (the Bellman said) saved them from wreck,
    Though none of the sailors knew how.

There was one who was famed for the number of things
    He forgot when he entered the ship:
His umbrella, his watch, all his jewels and rings,
    And the clothes he had bought for the trip.

He had forty-two boxes, all carefully packed,
    With his name painted clearly on each:
But, since he omitted to mention the fact,
    They were all left behind on the beach.

The loss of his clothes hardly mattered, because
    He had seven coats on when he came,
With three pairs of boots—but the worst of it was,
    He had wholly forgotten his name.

He would answer to "Hi!" or to any loud cry,
    Such as "Fry me!" or "Fritter my wig!"
To "What-you-may-call-um!" or "What-was-his-name!"
    But especially "Thing-um-a-jig!"

While, for those who preferred a more forcible word,
    He had different names from these:
His intimate friends called him "Candle-ends,"
    And his enemies "Toasted-cheese."

"His form is ungainly—his intellect small—"
    (So the Bellman would often remark)
"But his courage is perfect! And that, after all,
    Is the thing that one needs with a Snark."

He would joke with hyaenas, returning their stare
   With an impudent wag of the head:
And he once went a walk, paw-in-paw, with a bear,
   "Just to keep up its spirits," he said.

He came as a Baker: but owned, when too late—
    And it drove the poor Bellman half-mad—
He could only bake Bridecake—for which, I may state,
    No materials were to be had.

The last of the crew needs especial remark,
    Though he looked an incredible dunce:
He had just one idea—but, that one being "Snark,"
    The good Bellman engaged him at once.

He came as a Butcher: but gravely declared,
    When the ship had been sailing a week,
He could only kill Beavers. The Bellman looked scared,
    And was almost too frightened to speak:

But at length he explained, in a tremulous tone,
    There was only one Beaver on board;
And that was a tame one he had of his own,
    Whose death would be deeply deplored.

The Beaver, who happened to hear the remark,
    Protested, with tears in its eyes,
That not even the rapture of hunting the Snark
    Could atone for that dismal surprise!

It strongly advised that the Butcher should be
    Conveyed in a separate ship:
But the Bellman declared that would never agree
    With the plans he had made for the trip:

Navigation was always a difficult art,
    Though with only one ship and one bell:
And he feared he must really decline, for his part,
    Undertaking another as well.

The Beaver's best course was, no doubt, to procure
　　A second-hand dagger-proof coat—
So the Baker advised it—and next, to insure
　　Its life in some Office of note:

This the Banker suggested, and offered for hire
　　(On moderate terms), or for sale,
Two excellent Policies, one Against Fire,
　　And one Against Damage From Hail.

Yet still, ever after that sorrowful day,
　　Whenever the Butcher was by,
The Beaver kept looking the opposite way,
　　And appeared unaccountably shy.

Fit the Second

The Bellman's Speech

The Bellman himself they all praised to the skies—
    Such a carriage, such ease and such grace!
Such solemnity, too! One could see he was wise,
    The moment one looked in his face!

He had bought a large map representing the sea,
    Without the least vestige of land:
And the crew were much pleased when they found it to be
    A map they could all understand.

What's the good of Mercator's North Poles and Equators,
    Tropics, Zones, and Meridian Lines?"
So the Bellman would cry: and the crew would reply
    "They are merely conventional signs!

"Other maps are such shapes, with their islands and capes!
    But we've got our brave Captain to thank"
(So the crew would protest) "that he's bought us the best—
    A perfect and absolute blank!"

This was charming, no doubt: but they shortly found out
    That the Captain they trusted so well
Had only one notion for crossing the ocean,
    And that was to tingle his bell.

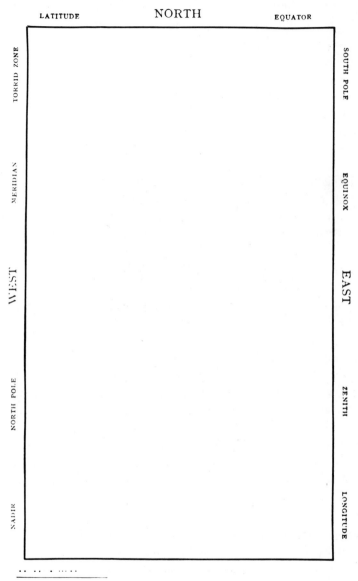

OCEAN-CHART.

He was thoughtful and grave—but the orders he gave
    Were enough to bewilder a crew.
When he cried "Steer to starboard, but keep her head larboard!"
    What on earth was the helmsman to do?

Then the bowsprit got mixed with the rudder sometimes:
    A thing, as the Bellman remarked,
That frequently happens in tropical climes,
    When a vessel is, so to speak, "snarked."

But the principal failing occurred in the sailing,
    And the Bellman, perplexed and distressed,
Said he *had* hoped, at least, when the wind blew due East,
    That the ship would *not* travel due West!

But the danger was past—they had landed at last,
    With their boxes, portmanteaus, and bags:
Yet at first sight the crew were not pleased with the view,
    Which consisted of chasms and crags.

The Bellman perceived that their spirits were low,
    And repeated in musical tone
Some jokes he had kept for a season of woe—
    But the crew would do nothing but groan.

He served out some grog with a liberal hand,
    And bade them sit down on the beach:
And they could not but own that their Captain looked grand,
    As he stood and delivered his speech.

"Friends, Romans, and countrymen, lend me your ears!"
    (They were all of them fond of quotations:
So they drank to his health, and they gave him three cheers,
    While he served out additional rations).

"We have sailed many months, we have sailed many weeks,
    (Four weeks to the month you may mark),
But never as yet ('tis your Captain who speaks)
    Have we caught the least glimpse of a Snark!

*We have sailed many weeks, we have sailed many days,
    (Seven days to the week I allow),
But a Snark, on the which we might lovingly gaze,
    We have never beheld till now!

"Come, listen, my men, while I tell you again
    The five unmistakable marks
By which you may know, wheresoever you go,
    The warranted genuine Snarks.

"Let us take them in order. The first is the taste,
    Which is meagre and hollow, but crisp:
Like a coat that is rather too tight in the waist,
    With a flavour of Will-o-the-wisp.

"Its habit of getting up late you'll agree
    That it carries too far, when I say
That it frequently breakfasts at five-o'clock tea,
    And dines on the following day.

"The third is its slowness in taking a jest,
    Should you happen to venture on one,
It will sigh like a thing that is deeply distressed:
    And it always looks grave at a pun.

"The fourth is its fondness for bathing-machines,
    Which it constantly carries about,
And believes that they add to the beauty of scenes—
    A sentiment open to doubt.

"The fifth is ambition. It next will be right
   To describe each particular batch:
Distinguishing those that have feathers, and bite,
   From those that have whiskers, and scratch.

"For, although common Snarks do no manner of harm,
   Yet, I feel it my duty to say,
Some are Boojums—" The Bellman broke off in alarm,
   For the Baker had fainted away.

Fit the Third
The Baker's Tale

They roused him with muffins—they roused him with ice—
   They roused him with mustard and cress—
They roused him with jam and judicious advice—
   They set him conumdrums to guess.

When at length he sat up and was able to speak,
   His sad story he offered to tell;
And the Bellman cried "Silence! Not even a shriek!"
   And excitedly tingled his bell.

There was silence supreme! Not a shriek, not a scream,
   Scarcely even a howl or a groan,
As the man they called "Ho!" told his story of woe
   In an antediluvian tone.

"My father and mother were honest, though poor——"
   "Skip all that!" cried the Bellman in haste.
"If it once becomes dark, there's no chance of a Snark—
   We have hardly a minute to waste!"

"I skip forty years," said the Baker, in tears,
   "And proceed without further remark
To the day when you took me aboard of your ship
   To help you in hunting the Snark.

"A dear uncle of mine (after whom I was named)
   Remarked, when I bade him farewell——"
"Oh, skip your dear uncle!" the Bellman exclaimed,
   As he angrily tingled his bell.

"He remarked to me then," said that mildest of men,
   " 'If your Snark be a Snark, that is right:
Fetch it home by all means—you may serve it with greens,
   And it's handy for striking a light.

" 'You may seek it with thimbles—and seek it with care;
   You may hunt it with forks and hope;
You may threaten its life with a railway-share;
   You may charm it with smiles and soap——' "

("That's exactly the method," the Bellman bold
   In a hasty parenthesis cried,
"That's exactly the way I have always been told
   That the capture of Snarks should be tried!")

" 'But oh, beamish nephew, beware of the day,
   If your Snark be a Boojum! For then
You will softly and suddenly vanish away,
   And never be met with again!'

"It is this, it is this that oppresses my soul,
    When I think of my uncle's last words:
And my heart is like nothing so much as a bowl
    Brimming over with quivering curds!

"It is this, it is this——" "We have heard that before!"
    The Bellman indignantly said.
And the Baker replied "Let me say it once more.
    It is this, it is this that I dread!

"I engage with the Snark—every night after dark—
    In a dreamy delirious fight:
I serve it with greens in those shadowy scenes,
    And I use it for striking a light:

"But if ever I meet with a Boojum, that day,
    In a moment (of this I am sure),
I shall softly and suddenly vanish away—
    And the notion I cannot endure!"

Fit the Fourth
The Hunting

The Bellman looked uffish, and wrinkled his brow.
    "If only you'd spoken before!
It's excessively awkward to mention it now,
    With the Snark, so to speak, at the door!

"We should all of us grieve, as you well may believe,
    If you never were met with again—
But surely, my man, when the voyage began,
    You might have suggested it then?

"It's excessively awkward to mention it now—
    As I think I've already remarked."
And the man they called "Hi!" replied, with a sigh,
    "I informed you the day we embarked.

"You may charge me with murder—or want of sense—
    (We are all of us weak at times):
But the slightest approach to a false pretence
    Was never among my crimes!

"I said it in Hebrew—I said it in Dutch—
    I said it in German and Greek:
But I wholly forgot (and it vexes me much)
    That English is what you speak!"

" 'Tis a pitiful tale," said the Bellman, whose face
    Had grown longer at every word:
"But, now that you've stated the whole of your case,
    More debate would be simply absurd.

"The rest of my speech" (he explained to his men)
    "You shall hear when I've leisure to speak it.
But the Snark is at hand, let me tell you again!
    'Tis your glorious duty to seek it!

"To seek it with thimbles, to seek it with care:
    To pursue it with forks and hope;
To threaten its life with a railway-share;
    To charm it with smiles and soap!

"For the Snark's a peculiar creature, that won't
    Be caught in a commonplace way.
Do all that you know, and try all that you don't:
    Not a chance must be wasted to-day!

"For England expects—I forbear to proceed:
  'Tis a maxim tremendous, but trite:
And you'd best be unpacking the things that you need
  To rig yourselves out for the fight."

Then the Banker endorsed a blank cheque (which he crossed),
  And changed his loose silver for notes.
The Baker with care combed his whiskers and hair,
  And shook the dust out of his coats.

The Boots and the Broker were sharpening a spade—
  Each working the grindstone in turn:
But the Beaver went on making lace, and displayed
  No interest in the concern:

Though the Barrister tried to appeal to its pride,
  And vainly proceeded to cite
A number of cases, in which making laces
  Had been proved an infringement of right.

The maker of Bonnets ferociously planned
  A novel arrangement of bows:
While the Billiard-marker with quivering hand
  Was chalking the tip of his nose.

But the Butcher turned nervous, and dressed himself fine,
  With yellow kid gloves and a ruff—
Said he felt it exactly like going to dine,
  Which the Bellman declared was all "stuff."

"Introduce me, now there's a good fellow," he said,
  "If we happen to meet it together!"
And the Bellman, sagaciously nodding his head,
  Said, "That must depend on the weather."

The Beaver went simply galumphing about,
    At seeing the Butcher so shy:
And even the Baker, though stupid and stout,
    Made an effort to wink with one eye.

"Be a man!" said the Bellman in wrath, as he heard
    The Butcher beginning to sob.
"Should we meet with a Jubjub, that desperate bird,
    We shall need all our strength for the job!"

Fit the Fifth

The Beaver's Lesson

They sought it with thimbles, they sought it with care;
    They pursued it with forks and hope;
They threatened its life with a railway-share;
    They charmed it with smiles and soap.

Then the Butcher contrived an ingenious plan
    For making a separate sally;
And had fixed on a spot unfrequented by man,
    A dismal and desolate valley.

But the very same plan to the Beaver occurred:
    It had chosen the very same place:
Yet neither betrayed, by a sign or a word,
    The disgust that appeared in his face.

Each thought he was thinking of nothing but "Snark"
    And the glorious work of the day;
And each tried to pretend that he did not remark
    That the other was going that way.

But the valley grew narrow and narrower still,
    And the evening got darker and colder,
Till (merely from nervousness, not from good will)
    They marched along shoulder to shoulder.

Then a scream, shrill and high, rent the shuddering sky,
    And they knew that some danger was near:
The Beaver turned pale to the tip of its tail,
    And even the Butcher felt queer.

He thought of his childhood, left far far behind—
    That blissful and innocent state—
The sound so exactly recalled to his mind
    A pencil that squeaks on a slate!

" 'Tis the voice of the Jubjub!" he suddenly cried.
    (This man, that they used to call "Dunce.")
"As the Bellman would tell you," he added with pride,
    "I have uttered that sentiment once.

" 'Tis the voice of the Jubjub! Keep count, I entreat;
    You will find I have told it you twice.
'Tis the song of the Jubjub! The proof is complete,
    If only I've stated it thrice."

The Beaver had counted with scrupulous care,
    Attending to every word:
But it fairly lost heart, and outgrabe in despair,
    When the third repetition occurred.

It felt that, in spite of all possible pains,
　　It had somehow contrived to lose count,
And the only thing now was to rack its poor brains
　　By reckoning up the amount.

"Two added to one—if that could but be done,"
　　It said, "with one's fingers and thumbs!"
Recollecting with tears how, in earlier years,
　　It had taken no pains with its sums.

"The thing can be done," said the Butcher, "I think.
　　The thing must be done, I am sure.
The thing shall be done! Bring me paper and ink,
　　The best there is time to procure."

The Beaver brought paper, portfolio, pens,
　　And ink in unfailing supplies:
While strange creepy creatures came out of their dens,
　　And watched them with wondering eyes.

So engrossed was the Butcher, he heeded them not,
　　As he wrote with a pen in each hand,
And explained all the while in a popular style
　　Which the Beaver could well understand.

"Taking Three as the subject to reason about—
　　A convenient number to state—
We add Seven, and Ten, and then multiply out
　　By One Thousand diminished by Eight.

"The result we proceed to divide, as you see,
　　By Nine Hundred and Ninety and Two.
Then subtract Seventeen, and the answer must be
　　Exactly and perfectly true.

"The method employed I would gladly explain,
    While I have it so clear in my head,
If I had but the time and you had but the brain—
    But much yet remains to be said.

"In one moment I've seen what has hitherto been
    Enveloped in absolute mystery,
And without extra charge I will give you at large
    A Lesson in Natural History."

In his genial way he proceeded to say
    (Forgetting all laws of propriety,
And that giving instruction, without introduction,
    Would have caused quite a thrill in Society),

"As to temper the Jubjub's a desperate bird,
    Since it lives in perpetual passion:
Its taste in costume is entirely absurd—
    It is ages ahead of the fashion:

"But it knows any friend it has met once before:
    It never will look at a bribe:
And in charity-meetings it stands at the door,
    And collects—though it does not subscribe.

"Its flavour when cooked is more exquisite far
    Than mutton, or oysters, or eggs:
(Some think it keeps best in an ivory jar,
    And some, in mahogany kegs:)

"You boil it in sawdust: you salt it in glue:
    You condense it with locusts and tape:
Still keeping one principal object in view—
    To preserve its symmetrical shape."

The Butcher would gladly have talked till next day,
    But he felt that the Lesson must end,
And he wept with delight in attempting to say
    He considered the Beaver his friend.

While the Beaver confessed, with affectionate looks
    More eloquent ever than tears,
It had learned in ten minutes far more than all books
    Would have taught it in seventy years.

They returned hand-in-hand, and the Bellman, unmanned
    (For a moment) with noble emotion,
Said "This amply repays all the wearisome days
    We have spent on the billowy ocean!"

Such friends, as the Beaver and Butcher became,
    Have seldom if ever been known;
In winter or summer, 'twas always the same—
    You could never meet either alone.

And when quarrels arose—as one frequently finds
    Quarrels will, spite of every endeavour—
The song of the Jubjub recurred to their minds,
    And cemented their friendship for ever!

Fit the Sixth

The Barrister's Dream

They sought it with thimbles, they sought it with care;
    They pursued it with forks and hope;
They threatened its life with a railway-share;
    They charmed it with smiles and soap.

But the Barrister, weary of proving in vain
    That the Beaver's lace-making was wrong,
Fell asleep, and in dreams saw the creature quite plain
    That his fancy had dwelt on so long.

He dreamed that he stood in a shadowy Court,
    Where the Snark, with a glass in its eye,
Dressed in gown, bands, and wig, was defending a pig
    On the charge of deserting its sty.

The Witnesses proved, without error or flaw,
    That the sty was deserted when found:
And the Judge kept explaining the state of the law
    In a soft under-current of sound.

The indictment had never been clearly expressed,
    And it seemed that the Snark had begun,
And had spoken three hours, before any one guessed
    What the pig was supposed to have done.

The Jury had each formed a different view
    (Long before the indictment was read),
And they all spoke at once, so that none of them knew
    One word that the others had said.

"You must know—" said the Judge: but the Snark exclaimed "Fudge!
    That statute is obsolete quite!
Let me tell you, my friends, the whole question depends
    On an ancient manorial right.

"In the matter of Treason the pig would appear
    To have aided, but scarcely abetted:
While the charge of Insolvency fails, it is clear
    If you grant the plea 'never indebted.'

"The fact of Desertion I will not dispute:
    But its guilt, as I trust, is removed
(So far as relates to the costs of this suit)
    By the Alibi which has been proved.

"My poor client's fate now depends on your votes."
    Here the speaker sat down in his place,
And directed the Judge to refer to his notes
    And briefly to sum up the case.

But the Judge said he never had summed up before;
    So the Snark undertook it instead,
And summed it so well that it came to far more
    Than the Witnesses ever had said!

When the verdict was called for, the Jury declined,
  As the word was so puzzling to spell;
But they ventured to hope that the Snark wouldn't mind
  Undertaking that duty as well.

So the Snark found the verdict, although, as it owned,
  It was spent with the toils of the day:
When it said the word "GUILTY!" the Jury all groaned,
  And some of them fainted away.

Then the Snark pronounced sentence, the Judge being quite
  Too nervous to utter a word:
When it rose to its feet, there was silence like night
  And the fall of a pin might be heard.

"Transportation for life" was the sentence it gave,
  "And *then* to be fined forty pound."
The Jury all cheered, though the Judge said he feared
  That the phrase was not legally sound.

But their wild exultation was suddenly checked
  When the jailer informed them, with tears,
Such a sentence would have not the slightest effect,
  As the pig had been dead for some years.

The Judge left the Court, looking deeply disgusted:
  But the Snark, though a little aghast,
As the lawyer to whom the defence was intrusted,
  Went bellowing on to the last.

Thus the Barrister dreamed, while the bellowing seemed
  To grow every moment more clear:
Till he woke to the knell of a furious bell,
  Which the Bellman rang close at his ear.

Fit the Seventh

The Banker's Fate

They sought it with thimbles, they sought it with care;
  They pursued it with forks and hope;
They threatened its life with a railway-share;
  They charmed it with smiles and soap.

And the Banker, inspired with a courage so new
  It was matter for general remark,
Rushed madly ahead and was lost to their view
  In his zeal to discover the Snark.

But while he was seeking with thimbles and care,
  A Bandersnatch swiftly drew nigh
And grabbed at the Banker, who shrieked in despair,
  For he knew it was useless to fly.

He offered large discount—he offered a cheque
  (Drawn "to bearer") for seven-pounds-ten:
But the Bandersnatch merely extended its neck
  And grabbed at the Banker again.

Without rest or pause—while those frumious jaws
  Went savagely snapping around—
He skipped and he hopped, and he floundered and flopped,
  Till fainting he fell to the ground.

The Bandersnatch fled as the others appeared
    Led on by that fear-stricken yell:
And the Bellman remarked "It is just as I feared!"
    And solemnly tolled on his bell.

He was black in the face, and they scarcely could trace
    The least likeness to what he had been:
While so great was his fright that his waistcoat turned white—
    A wonderful thing to be seen!

To the horror of all who were present that day,
    He uprose in full evening dress,
And with senseless grimaces endeavoured to say
    What his tongue could no longer express.

Down he sank in a chair—ran his hands through his hair—
　　And chanted in mimsiest tones
Words whose utter inanity proved his insanity,
　　While he rattled a couple of bones.

"Leave him here to his fate—it is getting so late!"
　　The Bellman exclaimed in a fright.
"We have lost half the day. Any further delay,
　　And we shan't catch a Snark before night!"

Fit the Eighth
The Vanishing

They sought it with thimbles, they sought it with care;
　　They pursued it with forks and hope;
They threatened its life with a railway-share;
　　They charmed it with smiles and soap.

They shuddered to think that the chase might fail,
　　And the Beaver, excited at last,
Went bounding along on the tip of its tail,
　　For the daylight was nearly past.

"There is Thingumbob shouting!" the Bellman said.
　　"He is shouting like mad, only hark!
He is waving his hands, he is wagging his head,
　　He has certainly found a Snark!"

They gazed in delight, while the Butcher exclaimed
  "He was always a desperate wag!"
They beheld him—their Baker—their hero unnamed—
  On the top of a neighbouring crag,

Erect and sublime, for one moment of time.
  In the next, that wild figure they saw
(As if stung by a spasm) plunge into a chasm,
  While they waited and listened in awe.

"It's a Snark!" was the sound that first came to their ears,
  And seemed almost too good to be true.
Then followed a torrent of laughter and cheers:
  Then the ominous words "It's a Boo—"

Then, silence. Some fancied they heard in the air
  A weary and wandering sigh
That sounded like "—jum!" but the others declare
  It was only a breeze that went by.

They hunted till darkness came on, but they found
  Not a button, or feather, or mark,
By which they could tell that they stood on the ground
  Where the Baker had met with the Snark.

In the midst of the word he was trying to say,
  In the midst of his laughter and glee,
He had softly and suddenly vanished away—
  For the Snark *was* a Boojum, you see.

THE END

Notes on the Poems

Making a selection of Lewis Carroll's verse necessarily entails more than a choice of poems, for in many instances there are a number of versions of the same poem. Dodgson was likely to revise a poem, delete a stanza here or there—or add a few stanzas, change a word, a line; the first or second publication is often at variance with that found in collections today. Biographers and compilers have often assigned titles to verses which Dodgson himself did not name. Complications further arise from typographical errors blindly repeated. Publishers and editors vary in their reprints of the poems.

A selection of poems would be virtually impossible, with attention to these changes, without the research and publications of Roger Lancelyn Green, most particularly *The Lewis Carroll Handbook, Being a New Version of A Handbook of the Literature of the Rev. C. L. Dodgson* by Sidney Herbert Williams and Falconer Madan, and the two volumes of Lewis Carroll *Diaries* edited by Green. The works of Stuart Dodgson Collingwood, Evelyn Hatch, Derek Hudson, Langford Reed, Florence Becker Lennon, and Martin Gardner, as well as articles and pamphlets by Horace Gregory, J. B. Shaw, and Morton N. Cohen, to mention only a few, have been most helpful. Special thanks are due to the personnel of the U.C.L.A. Research and Special Collections libraries for their help in making available source material.

Ultimately, however, the final choice of the poems, and of the particular version of those poems, must rest with the editor, and these notes are intended to explain that choice. In a number of instances it seemed that a poem as originally published contained more spontaneity and humor than in later versions. Three versions of "Hiawatha's Photographing" have been printed; the two most often reprinted omit some of the most delightful passages, which deal with the photographic process that Dodgson employed and his parody of Longfellow's Indian names. The *Alice* poems appear here with Dodgson's final corrections as specified by Stanley Godman in *The Times Literary Supplement,* May 2, 1958, including the addition of a comma to the penultimate stanza of "Jabberwocky" which, curiously enough changes the spirit of the line: "And, hast thou slain the Jabberwock?"

Carroll's serious poetry, that which was published early and incorporated later into *Phantasmagoria* (1869) and *Three Sunsets* (1898), has not been included in this volume. It is for the most part cloyingly sentimental and far overshadowed by his humorous verse. Similarly the early verse which he wrote and copied into family magazines is of great interest to the Carroll scholar, but does not measure up to his later work. In all cases, titles are used when the author intended them; otherwise the poems are identified by their first lines.

Section I includes verse from *Alice in Wonderland* and *Through the Looking-Glass, and What Alice Found There.* Of the sixteen poems, twelve are parodies, imitations or burlesques, here noted:

"How doth the little crocodile" is a parody of Isaac Watts's "Against Idleness and Mischief."

"Twinkle, twinkle, little bat!" is a parody of Jane Taylor's "The Star."

"Speak roughly to your little boy" parodies "Speak Gently" by David Bates, although there is some evidence that the original poem was written by G. W. Langford. Scholars are still weighing the evidence on this point.

" 'You are old, father William,' the young man said" is a biting parody of Robert Southey's poem "The Old Man's Comforts and How He Gained Them."

" 'Will you walk a little faster?' said a whiting to a snail," parodies the first line of Mary Howitt's "The Spider and the Fly." Carroll's rhythms and chorus are a distinct improvement on Howitt.

" 'Tis the voice of the Lobster: I heard him declare" is a parody of "The Sluggard" by Isaac Watts.

"Turtle Soup" is a parody of a song written by James M. Sayles, "Star of the Evening." Dodgson heard the Liddell sisters sing this on August 1, 1862, as he recorded in his diary.

"They told me you had been to her" is another version of a verse written earlier by Dodgson, "She's all my Fancy painted Him," published in *The Comic Times,* September 8, 1855. In its original publication it is a parody of another popular song, "Alice Gray" by William Mee. Another parody of this song, and a closer one, is the poem "Disillusionised."

"Jabberwocky" is based on a stanza which Carroll, at twenty-three, copied into *Mischmasch,* a family magazine, which he wrote for his brothers and sisters. This "Stanza of Anglo-Saxon Poetry" reads as follows, with the same bewildering punctuation which Dodgson himself used:

Stanza of Anglo-Saxon Poetry

TWAS BRYLLG & Y^E SLYTHY TOVES
DID GYRE AND GYMBLE IN Y^E WABE:
ALL MIMSY WERE Y^E BOROGOVES;
AND Y^E MOME RATHS OUTGRABE.

This curious fragment reads thus in modern characters:

TWAS BRYLLG, AND THE SLYTHY TOVES
DID GYRE AND GYMBLE IN THE WABE:
ALL MIMSY WERE THE BOROGOVES;
AND THE MOME RATHS OUTGRABE.

The meanings of the words are as follows:

BRYLLG. (derived from the verb to BRYL or BROIL) "the time of broiling dinner, i.e. the close of the afternoon"

SLYTHY (compounded of SLIMY AND LITHE). "smooth and active.

TOVE a species of Badger. They had smooth white hair, long hind legs, and short horns like a stag. lived chiefly on cheese

GYRE verb (derived from GYAOUR or GIAOUR, "a dog") "to scratch like a dog"

GYMBLE (whence GIMBLET) to screw out holes in anything

WABE (derived from the verb to SWAB or SOAK) "the side of hill. (from its being *soaked* by the rain)

MIMSY (whence MIMSERABLE and MISERABLE) "unhappy

BOROGOVE An extinct kind of Parrot. They had no wings beaks turned up, and made their nests under sun-dials   lived on veal

MOME (hence SOLEMOME SOLEMONE and SOLEMN) grave"

RATH A species of land turtle   Head erect   mouth like a shark the fore legs curved out so that the animal walked on it's knees. smooth green body   lived on swallows and oysters

OUTGRABE. past tense of the verb to OUTGRIBE (it is connected with the old verb to GRIKE or SHRIKE, from which are derived "shriek" and "creak") "squeaked"

Hence the literal English of the passage is;

"It was evening, and the smooth active badgers were scratching and boring holes in the hill side. all unhappy were the parrots, and the grave turtles squeaked out"

There were probably sun dials on the top of the hill, and the "borogoves were afraid that their nests would be undermined The hill was probably full of the nests of "raths", which ran out squeaking with fear on hearing the "toves" scratching outside This is an obscure, but yet deeply affecting relic of ancient Poetry.

Croft 1855 Ed

"The Walrus and the Carpenter" is thought by some to be a parody of Thomas Hood's "The Dream of Eugene Aram," both in meter and spirit.

"In Winter, when the fields are white" has been mentioned by J. B. Shaw as a parody of Longfellow's "Excelsior." There is nothing save a common meter to link the two in the present editor's opinion, and it is far more likely that "Excelsior" was parodied loosely by Dodgson in his "Lays of Sorrow, No. 1" in the first stanza, where

> The day was wet, the rain fell souse
>   Like jars of strawberry jam, a
> Sound was heard in the old henhouse,
>   A beating of a hammer.
> Of stalwart form, and visage warm,
>   Two youths were seen within it,
> Splitting up an old tree into perches for their poultry
>   At a hundred strokes a minute.

"The Aged Aged Man" is a composite parody. The situation parodies that of Wordsworth's "Resolution and Independence." An earlier version of "The Aged, Aged Man," "Upon the Lonely Moor," appeared in *The Train,* October 1856. The meter and form parody Thomas Moore's "My Heart and Lute."

"Hush-a-by lady, in Alice's lap!" is a parody of "Rock-a-bye-baby on the tree top."

"To the Looking-Glass world it was Alice that said" is a parody of Sir Walter Scott's "Bonnie Dundee."

Section II includes most of the verses from *Sylvie and Bruno* and *Sylvie and Bruno Concluded.* Two of the poems here are parodies: "King Fisher courted Lady Bird" which parodies the medieval court ballad, which was being revived at the time; and "In stature the Manlet was dwarfish" which parodies the style and meter of Algernon Charles Swinburne's "Dolores."

"He thought he saw an elephant" is written in a form originated by Carroll, called the Waterford.

Section III is a selection of some of Carroll's parodies and humorous verse.

"Hiawatha's Photographing," first published in *The Train* in 1857, has been reprinted in three versions. This is the original version, chosen because it retains the lines pertaining to the photographic process of the time, the passage making fun of Indian names (both omitted in later versions) and the interesting allusion to Texas and the United States at the end. Dodgson's love of photography, in spite of its obvious frustrations, is well expressed in this parody—indeed, he has even imitated the meter in the prose introduction!

"Lorenzo dwelt at Heighington" is from a story "The Legend of Scotland," written for the Longley children in 1858, but published posthumously in 1899.

"A Sea-Dirge" was first published in *College Rhymes* in 1860. A humorous contradiction to Dodgson's own love of the sea, it is here included in its first version, as later reprints omit the last two stanzas.

"Disillusionised," or "Disillusioned," was first published in *College Rhymes* in 1862. The original title may have been a typographical error, but it has been given here as written. It is usually reprinted with the second stanza omitted, and oftentimes with the title "My Fancy." It is a parody of sorts of William Mee's "Alice Gray," a popular song of the period.

"Ye Carpette Knyghte" was published in *The Train* in 1856. It is one of a number of poems written by Carroll in this style. "Ye Fattale Cheyse," an earlier poem that he contributed to *The Rectory Umbrella,* is also of this genre.

"Poeta Fit, Non Nascitur" was published in *College Rhymes* in 1862. This is the *Rhyme? and Reason?* version which varies only slightly from the original in punctuation.

Section IV includes Carroll's dedicatory poems, inscriptions, acrostics, double acrostics, puzzles and riddles.

"All in the golden afternoon" is the prefatory poem to *Alice's Adventures in Wonderland* (1865) and describes the circumstances surrounding the writing of the book, the boat trip, and the three Liddell sisters, Prima (Lorina), Secunda (Alice), and Tertia (Edith). It is dedicated to Alice Liddell.

"Child of the pure unclouded brow" is the prefatory poem to *Through the Looking-Glass, and What Alice Found There* (1872), and is also addressed to Alice Pleasance Liddell. Note that the third line of the last stanza contains the words "happy summer days," the last words of the book itself, and in the last line Dodgson has worked in Alice's middle name.

"A boat, beneath a sunny sky" is an acrostic poem which appears at the end of *Through the Looking-Glass*. The first letter of each line spells the name of Alice Pleasance Liddell.

"Girt with a boyish garb for boyish task," is the dedicatory poem to *The Hunting of the Snark* (1876). It is a double acrostic that spells the name of Gertrude Chataway in two ways; the first letter of each line spells her name as well as the first word of each stanza. Dodgson used this same poem with a few slight changes as the dedicatory poem in *Rhyme? and Reason?* (1883). The reference to the "boyish garb" points up the fact that as a child Gertrude was allowed to depart from the formal attire of little girls at the beach and run about in more comfortable clothes.

"Is all our Life, then, but a dream" is the prefatory poem to *Sylvie and Bruno* (1889), which was dedicated to Isa Bowman whose name is spelled by the first letter in each line. Isa was the sister of Maggie Bowman and acted the part of Alice on the stage in 1888. She wrote about Dodgson in a book, *Isa Bowman's Story of Lewis Carroll* in 1899.

"Cipher-Poem" was sent to Edith Argles in a letter dated April 29, 1868. It is a parody of Carroll's own parody of the Mary Howitt poem. Lily was a dog, and Dodgson also mentions Edith's sister Dolly in the poem.

"When .a.y and I.a told .a..ie they'd seen a" is a puzzle written for the Watson children, Mary, Ina, and Harriet. The editor has never seen the solution, but it is not difficult to fill in the missing words (knowing that Harriet's nickname was "Hartie"): i.e. Mary, Ina, Hartie, creature, wings, Hartie, fairy, Ina, Mary, Mary, Ina, Hartie, party, arithmetic.

"Puzzles from Wonderland" was written for the Cecil children and published in *Aunt Judy's Magazine* in 1870. Solutions signed "Eadgyth," were published in 1871, but there is no doubt that "Eadgyth" was Carroll himself. This is the original version.

"Thanks, thanks, fair Cousins, for your gift" was sent in a letter written by Dodgson to Mabel and Emily Kerr, May 20, 1881. Note that the first and last letters of the acrostic words spell both the names of Mabel and Emily and rhyme with the last word of the second line of each stanza.

The next two verses are acrostic inscriptions which Carroll wrote in copies of *The Hunting of the Snark:*

" 'Are you deaf, Father William?' the young man said." This is a parody on a parody and was written for Adelaide Paine whose name is spelled by the first letter of each line.

"Maidens! if you love the tale," was written for Minnie, Ella, and Emmie Drury whose names are also spelled by the first letter of each line. Dodgson wrote many other poems for the Drurys whom he first met on a railway trip.

Section V is Carroll's poem *The Hunting of the Snark,* whose meaning has been a never-ending quest for message-seekers from its publication until today!

Index of Titles
and First Lines

"Will you trot a little quicker?"
said a Lily to a Fox, 95
"Will you walk a little faster?"
said a whiting to a snail, 20

Ye Carpette Knyghte, 79
"You are old, father William,"
the young man said, 16

ABOUT THE COMPILER

Myra Cohn Livingston was born in Omaha, Nebraska, and grew up in Los Angeles. She began writing poetry when she was very young and continued to do so as a student at Sarah Lawrence College. In addition to her work as poet and anthologist, Mrs. Livingston is especially interested in encouraging younger poets and is currently Poet in Residence for the Beverly Hills Unified School District, where she teaches creative writing. She also lectures at universities and colleges around the country. With her husband and their children—Josh, Jonas, and Jennie—she lives in Beverly Hills, California.

ABOUT THE ILLUSTRATIONS

The illustrations for this book are reproduced from the original editions of Lewis Carroll's works. John Tenniel was the most famous of the artists associated with Carroll; his illustrations for *Alice's Adventures in Wonderland* and *Through the Looking-Glass* appear on the title page of this book and on pages 1, 15, 16, 17, 18, 19, 21, 27, 29, 30, 32, 34, 37, and 151. The pictures from *Sylvie and Bruno* and *Sylvie and Bruno Concluded,* on pages 41, 42, 43, 44, 45, 46, 54, 59, 60, and 61, are by Harry Furniss. Selected illustrations by Arthur B. Frost from *Rhyme? and Reason?* appear on pages 65, 67, 69, 70, 72, 75, 80, and 84. Henry Holiday's illustrations for *The Hunting of the Snark* are on pages 111, 113, 115, 122, 127, 131, 134, 137, and 138. The pictures on pages 22 and 88 and the ornaments used on part titles throughout the book are taken from the illustrated manuscript of *Alice's Adventures Underground* which Lewis Carroll himself drew for Alice Liddell.